MIRACLES

Miracles Can Happen
Remarkable Stories

Phil Shirley

Hodder & Stoughton
LONDON SYDNEY AUCKLAND

Margaret, without whom . . .

and those who trusted me to write these stories. Thank you.

Copyright © Phil Shirley

First published in Great Britain 1996

The right of Phil Shirley to be identified as the Author of
the Work has been asserted by him in accordance with the
Copyright, Designs and Patents Act 1988.

10 9 8 7 6 5 4 3 2 1

British Library Cataloguing in Publication Data
A record for this book is available from the British Library

ISBN 0 340 65625 5

Printed and bound in Great Britain by
Cox & Wyman, Reading, Bucks.

Hodder and Stoughton Ltd
A Division of Hodder Headline PLC
338 Euston Road
London NW1 3BH

Contents

CONTENTS

❧ vi ❧

Introduction

I remember once meeting a professional miracle hunter. It was during a violent rainstorm in Texas. I was sitting in the departure lounge at Dallas-Forth Worth Airport, minding my own business, waiting to board a plane to Chicago.

It was the end of a long weekend. I'd been working south of Dallas on a story for a magazine and couldn't wait to escape the oppressive Texas humidity – the kind of sweltering heat that makes breathing hard work. The check-in clerk told me Chicago was heavy but ten degrees cooler.

I was just thankful for the air conditioning – and that I could sit there, sip the cool beer that was rapidly warming in the bottle in my hand, and wait for the storm clouds to roll away. I certainly wasn't in the mood for conversation.

It was then that he appeared, as if from nowhere, smiled a greeting and sat down next to me. And started to talk.

It turned out that he was a fellow journalist. *Too bad*, I thought, *we have something in common*. I really didn't want a full-scale, airport lounge, verbal exchange with this man. But he started talking anyway. Maybe I hadn't been staring hard enough – or perhaps *too* hard. He said he thought the storm would pass quickly enough for the flight to leave on time.

I looked out of the huge terminal windows at the torrential rain lashing the planes and pounding the ground. On the approach runway two jets stood stranded in the downpour. I swivelled to look at the clock on the wall, then turned back to my uninvited companion. 'It'll take a miracle,' I said.

He looked at me with a strange gleam in his eyes. 'And what do you know about miracles?'

I frowned, took another sip of beer, and shrugged my shoulders.

Then I got the full story. This man, in his mid-fifties, maybe older, had spent twenty years hunting miracles, investigating supernatural stories, for various newspapers and magazines – not to revel in them but to disprove them. He had even started work on a book, *Miraculous Lies*, and had become so cynical that his work had become a witch-hunt. 'I had lost my faith in God and in all the good things in this world,' he told me.

But that was before he had a massive heart attack – and died. 'There was nothing the doctors could do to save me,' he said. 'My heart simply exploded and I was certified dead on arrival at hospital. But my spirit was sent hurtling into eternity . . . toward a place I hadn't believed could exist.'

He told me that his sister was called to the mortuary to identify the body – he wasn't married – and the death certificate was issued the following day.

I just sat there, silent, doubting any of this was true, when he reached into his briefcase and pulled out the death certificate – his *own* death certificate – along with a newspaper cutting of an interview with the doctor who had pronounced him dead and later described his return to the land of the living as 'a miracle of Lazarus proportions'. You know Lazarus – the man Jesus raised from the dead.

I looked at him, wondering, mouth open, trying to be cool next to a former dead person. He looked at me, waiting for a reaction. I didn't know what to say.

The gleam in his eyes was brighter now. 'I went to heaven!' he said, sensing that I needed help piercing the fog swirling around in my mind. 'In between dying and suddenly sitting up on the mortuary slab, wondering where I was, I went to heaven. I was aware of the awesome presence of God, my creator. I heard his voice, so majestic and filled with compassion. He told me I had died before my time, and said I was to return with a new heart and renewed faith.'

I smiled at my companion and sat shaking my head. Not because I didn't believe him, but because suddenly I realised I was sitting in the presence of someone who had been given another shot at life, a second chance to believe in something greater than our one-dimensional, self-interested world.

Just then the announcement came over the public address informing us that the flight would be delayed because of the storm. He smiled at me. 'No miracle after all. But believe me, young man, they can and do happen.'

That is the message of this book. You won't find a death certificate among its pages, but I hope you will find encouragement and inspiration.

1

Bomb Blast

The bombs had done their worst. Shattered houses, broken men and women, sobbing children. Homes had been ripped apart, bodies lay crushed. Only the whimpering of the survivors was more distressing than the sight of the dead.

All night long surgeons had worked to repair and revive. The walking wounded stood in line, the less fortunate were carried to the makeshift surgery on stretchers, some slumped on boards and doors. Ambulance and motorcycle dispatch carried blood plasma from the depots through the fire and rubble. Firefighters sweated in the heat and choked on smoke. People searching for loved ones and friends sweated in fear and gulped back tears.

John Grady was eight years old. When the German fighter-bomber lunged toward London he was playing with a box of tin soldiers. He sat cross-legged on the bedroom floor lining up the toy men in single file before knocking them down like dominoes. His mother, Jane, stood in the front room of her terraced house, ironing. By the time the first siren howled it was already too late.

Spitfires shot down five of the German warplanes, two crashing outside the city. Another two were ripped apart by anti-aircraft guns. One of the raiders got through, twisting and turning, searching for an easy target. It came screaming out of the clouds, flying low before releasing its bombs. For many death was instant.

One of the bombs exploded in the street outside John's house, another blew the roof off the house next door. The blast threw his mother across the room, tossing her in the air like a rag doll.

Walls crumbled, windows and doors exploded. The living room ceiling caved in, burying Jane under an avalanche of plaster, bricks and timber. The boy was curled into a ball in the corner of the bedroom. The gaping hole in the floor had swallowed the bed. The fighter-bomber made another lunge, machine guns blazing. John screamed, clamping trembling hands over his ears to deaden the awful noise.

The raider made one last attack, raking the debris with bullets before banking away from the carnage and climbing up through the smoke and clouds. John waited, eyes shut tight, hands still over his ears. He waited for more bombs and bullets, frozen by fear and whispering: 'Jesus, save me. Jesus, save me. Keep us safe, save my mum, don't let her die.'

All through the attack the boy had prayed. Even when the house shook and the floor trembled violently, he did not stop whispering to God. The bedroom ceiling twisted and cracked and finally caved in, showering the room with debris. John flinched in terror as plaster and timber rained down. He cried out loud when another bomb exploded outside, shattering the glass in the windows. But he kept praying. 'Keep us safe, Lord, keep us safe. God, keep us alive. Please make it stop, make it stop.'

And it did stop. When all the killing had been done and when the street lay in ruins, all was quiet again. Only then did John stop praying. And then he wept. He cried and cried, and his tiny body trembled. He remained curled up in the corner, not daring to move, not daring even to open his eyes.

When he took his hands from his ears the silence seemed more deafening than the exploding bombs. Soon the broken building creaked and groaned. Debris shifted, crumbled and fell. In the distance a siren whined. From somewhere outside came shouts, then screams.

Slowly John opened his eyes, squinting in the darkness, ready to snap them shut again as flames from a burning house across the street cast frightening shapes on his wall. Dust and smoke filled the room. He could smell and taste it, and struggled to breathe.

He got up on to his knees, reaching out his hand to feel the floor in front of him, the wall behind. Bravely, he stood, then slowly moved sideways, his back pressed against the wall. He thought of his mother but could not call out her name.

Another step, and another, but then there was no more floor and John was falling through the darkness, his young mind gripped with fear.

Suddenly strong hands broke his fall. Then he was being carried through the rubble that had been his home and out into the cool night air. Gently, the hands lowered him, setting him back on his feet and steadying him, palms reassuringly flat on his back. At last John felt safe. But when he turned around he was alone.

It was eight in the morning when the workmen started digging a long, common grave for the dead. Rescuers were picking through the rubble, searching for survivors. A soldier found John inside the bombed house. The boy was on his knees, clawing through the debris with his bare hands. 'My mother's in here,' he told the soldier. 'She's not dead, she's in here,' John screamed and kicked as the soldier dragged him away.

'Where did you find him?' a sergeant asked.

The soldier had to use all his strength to keep the boy from running back into what was left of his home. 'In the end house,' he said. 'He hasn't got a scratch on him. He was trying to find his mother . . .'

The sergeant shook his head. 'That side of the street took the worst of it. It's a wonder the kid survived.'

The soldier nodded. 'He says he was upstairs and fell through a hole in the floor. Says someone caught him and carried him outside.'

'Who?'

The soldier shrugged. 'He doesn't know.' He looked at John's tear-streaked face. 'He must have got out on his own.'

The sergeant thought for a moment. 'Take him over to the church hall. There are women over there; they'll look after him.'

Jane sat slumped on a pew, crying. Another woman held her, stroking her hair, comforting her.

'They wouldn't let me look for him,' Jane muttered. 'Said it was too dangerous. No survivors, they said. No survivors. I was the only one. Oh, John . . .'

'It's amazing anyone got out alive,' said another woman.

Jane wiped her eyes. 'I don't remember much, just someone lifting me up and carrying me out. I don't know who it was. Took me out into the street and set me down. But when I looked there was no one there. No one at all.'

2

Paradise Springs

FAR WEST TEXAS, 1927

Ed Juan watched the clouds move across the desolate land. The racing shadows passed over him, over the desert hell. He turned and looked back at the ranch. Cloud shadows swooped across the white and sky blue house like some giant eagle whose wings cast terrifying shadows on its prey. He wished such a creature would dive down out of the clouds and tear John McCreery's head off. 'I hate you, McCreery, I hate you,' he croaked. His lips were cracked and his throat bone dry.

It was summer and all around the ranch the desert was burning. Outside Ed Juan's tiny shack John McCreery was fastening a big black padlock and chain on the hand-pump by the side of the well. He was cursing and swearing, sweat running down his leathery face. 'I'll teach you, I'll show you,' he hissed. 'You little grease monkey, stinking little greaser. I'll show you till your tongue shrivels up and drops out. No one crosses John McCreery, no one.'

Ed Juan's wife, Evita, could only feel sorry for the old man as she watched him clamp down the water pump. 'Don't curse him,' she urged her husband. 'Don't wish to kill him. Feel sorry for him, pray for his soul. John McCreery has the devil on his back.'

'He *is* the devil,' Ed Juan retorted as they lay together in the cool of the night. 'He deserves to die.'

Above them the stars shone through holes in the roof – a thousand eyes peering through the veil of night, watching the two poor Mexican workers sucking water from a rag, while across the ranch in his white and sky blue house the old man drank whiskey from a crystal glass.

John McCreery started torturing Ed Juan and Evita the day one of his prize saddlebreds died from a rattlesnake bite. It was Ed Juan's job to check for snakes on the ranch, especially in the horse boxes, and John McCreery blamed him when Alamo, a young chestnut stallion, was struck twice by a large cottonmouth. It was not Ed Juan's fault. One of the other Mexican workers had caught the snake to make money from its venom and had hidden it inside a sack in the barn. He had confessed after the horse died but John McCreery had already made up his mind to punish Ed Juan. He wanted to make him suffer.

'Why are you doing this to me, Mr McCreery?' Ed Juan asked. 'Haven't I been faithful to you? Am I not a good, honest worker – a friend, even?'

Light from the porch lantern shone on Ed Juan's face. John McCreery could see the cracks in the dry skin of the other man's lips. He could see pain in his eyes, too. 'It's not for you to question why,' the old man growled. 'If you don't like it you can leave.'

Ed Juan looked at the floor. Dry wind blew the lantern and the flickering light made patterns in the cooling sand swirling across the wooden boards. John McCreery stroked the barrel of the shotgun he was holding. It was loaded and aimed in the direction of a greasewood bush, barely visible a short distance from the house. In the sand beneath the bush a kangaroo rat was getting ready to emerge from its burrow. John McCreery was getting ready to blow its head off. 'You remind me of a rat,' he told Ed Juan, 'but you ain't clever like one. The rat burrows into the sand in the day and pulls the hole in after him, smart critter. He makes a water hole, wetted by his own breath. Damn smart.'

Ed Juan looked up. He saw John McCreery bring the gun up level, a bloodshot eye staring down its length. 'Where there is no water, he makes it anyway,' Ed Juan said to himself. He flinched as the shotgun barked, then watched as the old man strode over to the bush.

'Nailed him,' said John McCreery with satisfaction. 'Nailed him good and proper.'

Ed Juan started walking back to the shack. He knew there was no point in trying to reason with John McCreery and he didn't turn around when the old man shouted after him: 'You can use the well tomorrow night if you give me an honest day's work. Do you hear me, Juan? An honest day's work for an honest day's pay, I say. You little rat.'

The work was killing Ed Juan. His daily workload had doubled, sometimes tripled, since the horse had died. The old man would set impossible tasks and if they were not complete on time Ed Juan and Evita would go another day without water. Sometimes they would go three days before John McCreery unlocked the pump and let them fill two tin pails, for drinking, cooking and washing.

John McCreery knew Ed Juan and Evita were at his mercy. It was he who had taken them in, given Ed Juan a job, and provided a roof over their heads. And since his was the only ranch for many miles, he had been their only hope. 'Without me you wouldn't have survived,' he reminded Ed Juan. 'You came over the border looking for the American dream and I gave you a taste of it. Money, good food, a decent, God-fearing Texas life. Now it's this or nothing – you either do as I say or you can go back to your Mexican hell.'

Ed Juan knew there was no easy way out. If he and Evita left the ranch it was likely they would wind up half-dead, begging for food, living like animals in some bad place. 'We can't give up, we can't let him destroy us,' Evita told her husband. 'Remember when we first came to this ranch, when Elaine McCreery was alive and for the first time in our lives we had a place we could call home, food on the table, a future, something to live for? Well, we *still* have something to live for. We believe in God – we'll trust our future to him.'

John McCreery had always been a mean, cold-hearted man. Even before his wife Elaine died in the winter of '25 he used to give the ranch hands a hard time, making them sweat and grind all hours for a poor wage. But at least Elaine used to keep him in check, restrain his violent mood swings and cruel urges. When Ed Juan and Evita arrived at the ranch in the summer of 1922, John McCreery wanted to kill them; 'Tie them to their mules and turn them loose,' he said. 'Let the sun boil their brains and blister their skin.'

Elaine scolded him, as she often did during their thirty-year marriage, and offered the two weary Mexican travellers food and water. Later she asked the other ranch hands to clear the old storeroom so that Ed Juan and Evita had somewhere to rest. She pleaded with her husband to give Ed Juan a job and he reluctantly agreed.

Elaine took Evita under her wing, teaching the pretty young Mexican girl to cook Texan style, and to play the piano. In exchange for jobs around the house she gave them food, and coal for the stove that kept the shack warm during the winter.

John McCreery hated it. He despised how Elaine treated the Mexicans so well – like fellow Texans. 'How could she?' he complained. It was a question he asked almost every day. But he never chastised his wife for her kindness. He loved her too much to do that.

Ed Juan and Evita almost drowned crossing the Rio Grande River, entering the United States illegally, two shadows in the night, slipping silently across *la frontera*, the border, where the Third World meets the First World, and the lure of the dollar draws men and women to confront the last geographical obstacle in their struggle toward a better life. Ed Juan's younger brother Francisco died during the crossing. Dragged along in a strong current, he smashed his head on a rock and disappeared beneath the surface of the Rio Grande. Ed Juan watched him slip away and prayed that the river would release his spirit. He prayed, too, that he and Evita would have the strength to carry on.

Even though John McCreery hated Ed Juan, he could not fault his work, although he was never satisfied, never grateful for the extra effort, for the times when the wiry little Mexican would work the land from sunrise to sundown, only stopping to take a sip of water from his hip flask. For more than three years Ed Juan worked six days every week, resting on Sunday, church once in the morning and again in the evening.

Ed Juan and Evita were raised Catholics, but Elaine took Evita to a Baptist church the week before Christmas 1922, the year they came to the McCreery ranch, and the experience changed her. 'I found God in a tin church in the middle of a desert, I am so happy now,' she told Ed Juan on her return to the ranch following her very first visit. 'I have found my faith again. Now I know Jesus and it feels so good.'

When Elaine died, John McCreery cried for three days. They buried her in the desert behind the church. Evita threw a white satin rose on the coffin. Ed Juan felt numb because he knew hatred would fill the void created by her death. John McCreery drank whiskey during the funeral service and smashed the empty bottle against the church door. Ed Juan saw the haunted look in his eyes, and behind it a malevolent stare.

'If there is anything we can do . . .'

'Go to hell!' John McCreery snapped, kicking up a cloud of red dust as he staggered to his horse. 'That's what you can do – go to hell.'

Evita turned to Ed Juan. 'He doesn't mean it,' she whispered. 'He's hurting.'

'No, I am afraid you are wrong,' Ed Juan said. 'You don't know him like I do. The only good thing in his life has gone. Now he is all bad and everyone will suffer. Everyone.'

The words came back to Ed Juan that night, echoing in the deep places of his tired mind as he fell into his bed. Soon the red dust turned into a swarm of angry wasps, consuming him, but when he tried to run his legs felt like lead, and he could only crawl across the ground. Then the earth opened up beneath him and he looked down into the grave where Elaine McCreery's corpse lay – a watery grave, bubbling and spitting like a cauldron on a fire. He started falling and turned to cry out to Evita for help. It was then he saw that John McCreery had jumped after him, and he was clutching the broken whiskey bottle like a dagger. Even in his dreams his tormentor would not give up.

The room was spinning when he awoke. He sat bolt upright, bathed in cold sweat. He saw familiar shapes, the stars shining through the holes in the roof of the shack, and felt the softness of the mattress, and the moisture on his skin. He breathed deeply, slowly, tasting the chill in the night air. *Just a dream, only a dream.* He lay back, sliding closer to Evita. Her warmth was comforting and he felt safe beside her, safe from the nightmare, safe from the darkness.

He ran his tongue across his cracked, dry lips, then reached over and took the rag from Evita's open hand. It was the rag he had buried beneath the scorched desert to soak up moisture from the deeper earth where the burning rays of sun could not penetrate. It was still moist and he bit hard into the pungent material. *I'll get water today even if it kills me*, he thought. *I've done my work and I'll work even harder today to make sure John McCreery keeps his promise.*

He took the rag from his mouth and rubbed his nose in Evita's long black hair, smelling the sweet fragrance of the woman he loved. 'Don't worry, baby,' he whispered. 'I will not let your pretty lips cry out for water again. Ed Juan will see to that.'

The barbed wire shimmered in the heat. Ed Juan sat down on a rock and looked back along the half-mile stretch of fencing. It had taken him the best part of a day but he'd done it, and from where he sat it looked pretty good. His hands were cut from unwinding the wire and the cracks on his lips were worse than ever. There had been no water to fill a flask and Ed Juan had stopped himself from dehydrating by sucking red fruit from a prickly pear cactus. The white spines and the brown barbs hurt his fingers more than the steel spikes on the wire, but he had no choice. John McCreery had seen to that. But even in his pain Ed Juan managed a wry smile as he peeled another fruit. *I can't wait to see the look on the old man's face*, he mused. *He thought I would not be able to lay down a half-mile of fence. But he will have to unchain the water pump now – and if he doesn't, I will kill him anyway and take all the water I need.*

John McCreery was sitting in a chair on the porch of his white and sky blue house when Ed Juan rode through the ranch gates. The old man watched intently as the Mexican dismounted, took the reins over the horse's head and looped them around the fence in front of the shack. He had a mule in tow and released its lead rope from the saddle of the horse and led it over to the house. John McCreery stood up when Ed Juan reached the porch steps. 'Wire spools are empty, Mr McCreery,' he said glancing at the two cardboard reels fastened on to the mule's pack.

'I know you've laid down the whole half-mile,' the old man answered. 'I rode out along the trail 'bout two hours ago. Saw the wire running in a straight line down past the old steer run. I thought I told you to run it south along the bottom canyon ridge.' John McCreery tapped his boot on the top step. He saw Ed Juan's face change. It reminded him of a thunder sky, and there was thunder in Ed Juan's heart.

The Mexican flew up the porch steps, pinning John McCreery to the screen door of the house before the pair of them crashed through and on to the kitchen floor. Ed Juan had both hands around John McCreery's neck and was squeezing the life out of the old man when Evita ran into the room. Grabbing her husband's hair, she yelled for him to stop. Ed Juan got to his feet and watched John McCreery as he sat up and felt his throat. Ed Juan's heart was pounding, but the old man looked unbelievably calm. He glanced up at the Mexican. 'No more water for a week,' he said. 'I hope you both die of thirst.'

Back at the shack Ed Juan was trembling. 'I should have killed him,' he growled. 'You should not have stopped me – he deserves to die.'

'And then what? A place in the execution line? Is that what you want, Ed Juan? Do you want to lose your life, lose me?' There were tears in Evita's dark eyes. 'Go ahead, take a shovel, take a knife. Go into that house and kill John McCreery. Go, Ed Juan – what are you waiting for?'

Ed Juan closed his eyes. He had pain in his chest; a burning anger. He wanted to scream, but instead he cried out: 'I can't take any more, I can't take it! Why, why, why? Why is he doing this to us? What have we done to deserve it? Oh, God, help us! Stop this persecution – please, God, please.'

'He will, Ed Juan,' Evita assured him. 'He will help us, you will see. You will know God's goodness.' She held Ed Juan tighter than she had ever held him before, until his sobbing stopped and night fell around the shack, the stars once again shining through the holes in the roof. 'Angels are watching over us,' she whispered, but Ed Juan did not hear. He was asleep.

It had been two days since Ed Juan had attacked John McCreery, and the old man was carrying out his threat. There was no way Ed Juan could get water from the well. The pump was shackled down and John McCreery spent most of the day and night sitting on his front porch with a shotgun in his hand ready to shoot the first person who tried anything. In the beginning, when John McCreery first cut off the water supply, the other ranch hands had shared their rations with Ed Juan and Evita. But now there was no one to help them. The old man had got rid of everyone else. They were prisoners, with one hundred miles of barren land in every direction and the threat of a lingering death in the desert was as forbidding as any prison wall. Without water they could not even consider leaving.

'Where would we go, even if we could get away?' Evita asked. 'Back to Mexico? Back across the Rio Grande River? Do we wander through the desert hoping someone will show us mercy, take us in like Elaine McCreery did all those years ago? The church is just a ruin and no one else cares if we live or die. We have to stay here, we must trust in God.'

'But I cannot survive another day without water in this desert hell,' he said. 'I want to go out there and smash the chain off the pump and draw all the water we need.' Ed Juan was looking out of the shack window. 'He's not on the porch, he must be inside. Maybe I should go out and do it now.'

Evita squeezed his hand. 'He'll kill you,' she said. 'He will hear you and then shoot you. And then your brother's death will be for nothing.'

'You are wrong, Evita. I will do this thing for Francisco, I will stand up to John McCreery and take the water.'

Ed Juan made for the door but Evita stepped in front of him, clasping his face in her hands. 'What is your dream?' she asked, her voice trembling. 'Why did you risk everything to come to this place?'

There was no answer. Ed Juan was silent, his eyes closed.

'Tell me, remind yourself,' she said, squeezing Ed Juan's face. 'Or have you lost your faith? Is that what it is? You are giving up, quitting?'

Ed Juan relaxed and smiled gently at his wife. 'I still have the dream,' he said. 'I still believe we can save enough money so that one day we can have a ranch of our own. I have not lost my faith, you know that.'

He placed his hands around Evita's narrow waist and kissed her gently on the lips. 'I don't pray to God as much as I should,' he told her. 'But I still believe in him and know that he hears our prayers. I am just afraid, Evita. I am afraid that John McCreery won't stop until we are dead.'

'I know Ed Juan, I feel your pain and sense your fear. But God will sustain us, he won't let us die of thirst, you will see. We almost have enough money now, just another six months, maybe less and we can leave this place. Remember the plan, remember how it is going to work?'

'Yes I know, I think about it almost every day.' He led Evita over to the bed and they sat on the edge, holding hands. 'We will go in the middle of the night, when it is cool,' he said, closing his eyes to imagine. 'We will take two horses and a mule but leave enough money to pay for them. We will fill barrels with water and strap them on the mule, then we will ride south following the Rio Grande River, maybe all the way down to the ocean, until we find a place where we can build a house and farm the land. Then we will . . . '

Evita placed two fingers over his lips. 'It will be wonderful,' she whispered. 'And it will happen, Ed Juan, our dream will come true, you will see. We must pray now, ask God to help us survive until the time is right to go.' She squeezed his hand and together they knelt by the side of the bed. Ed Juan rested his elbows on the mattress and held his head in his hands. Evita closed her eyes and bowed her head. They prayed and waited on God until the sun went down. When they had finished Ed Juan looked up toward heaven through the holes in the roof, and the stars in the night sky seemed to shine brighter than ever before.

John McCreery had risen early. The sun was just coming up over the mountains and the air was still cool and fresh. He had taken the lock and chain off the pump handle and was holding his head under a cold stream of water as he moved the wooden stock up and down. Ed Juan stood in the doorway of the shack. Evita was still asleep. The old man sensed he was being watched and turned to see Ed Juan leaning on the rotten timber frame. 'The water's good and fresh,' he shouted before taking a long drink. The water sprayed over his face and ran down his neck. Ed Juan watched a small river snake away from John McCreery's boots across the wooden boards around the base of the well, then disappear into the red earth.

'Come on, come and have some.' The old man stood up and beckoned Ed Juan. 'Forget what I said the other day, fetch a pail, fetch two pails. It's going to be hotter than ever today. A man could easily die out there.' He looked out at the desert, gazing south towards the bottom canyon ridge, where Ed Juan was going to lay down another line of barbed wire fencing. 'What are you waiting for?' John McCreery shouted, then smiled.

The old man sat on the wall of the well while Ed Juan pumped water into the second pail. He kept glancing at John McCreery, who was now stroking the beech stock of his shotgun. Evita was awake now and stood outside the shack, shielding her eyes from the morning sun. It was almost clear of the mountains now and shone more fiercely with every passing second. She watched Ed Juan finish filling the tin pail. She felt uneasy. The old man had a strange look in his eyes.

John McCreery stood up, pointing the gun at Ed Juan. 'Done?' he asked.

'Yes, sir, thank you,' Ed Juan answered, bending down to lift the two pails.

'Now, hang on a minute, boy,' John McCreery snorted. He took two steps toward the Mexican. 'Is that all the thanks I get?'

Evita started praying, silently. 'I said thank you. I – we – appreciate your kindness,' Ed Juan said.

'It's not enough,' John McCreery snapped. 'I want you down on your knees. Kiss my boots, show me just how grateful you are.'

Ed Juan released his grip on the pails. His fists were clenched and he squared up to the old man. Evita ran over. 'Walk away, Ed Juan, now,' she said calmly, squeezing her husband's shoulder.

'Better do what the little lady says.' John McCreery raised the gun higher so that the barrel was level with Ed Juan's chest.

Evita squeezed harder and Ed Juan backed off. The old man lashed out with his right boot and sent both pails tumbling over. All three watched the water spill out and drain into the ground. 'I want the fencing done by sunset,' he said. 'If it ain't I want you both off the ranch. Now go before I shoot you for trying to steal my water.'

The heat was so bad along bottom canyon ridge that Ed Juan thought he might pass out. If it hadn't been for the small amount of water he took with him in his hip flask that morning, he would surely have wound up face down in the dust by sundown. Evita had gone back for the pails after John McCreery had chained down the pump handle and returned to the house. There was water in both, barely a few mouthfuls, but it was enough to fill Ed Juan's flask by a quarter.

He finished the fencing and staggered back along the ridge to where he had tied the mule in the shade of a hanging rock. He felt sick, could not see straight, and instead of leading the animal back along the trail to the ranch, he slumped over its back, one leg dragging on the ground, the other jabbing the mule's side to keep it moving. By the time they reached the ranch, Ed Juan was semi-conscious and fell to the ground when the mule stopped outside the shack. John McCreery was sitting outside his house, drinking whiskey. He laughed as Evita dragged her husband inside.

'I'm dying,' Ed Juan gasped. He was lying face down on the bed, sucking a rag that Evita had soaked in the mule trough. The old man had forgot to empty it. Twice a day he would check to make sure the horses and mule had enough to drink, and then at night he would kick over the troughs so that the two Mexicans could not sneak a drink while he was sleeping.

He even tied a cow-bell to the chain on the pump handle so that he could hear anyone trying to draw water from the well. But now he was so full of whiskey that he did not see or hear Evita leave the shack and enter the barn. The troughs were almost empty anyway and the water filthy, but Ed Juan was dehydrated and he sucked hard on the rag, even though the rancid taste made him shudder. He was exhausted and fell into a deep sleep. Evita lay her head on his chest, placed the rag between her cracked lips and sucked gently. She felt Ed Juan's heart beating, and drifted away, lulled by the rhythm of the pulse.

Evita was woken by an unfamiliar sound. At first she did not know what it was, but gradually the noise became clearer. She sat up, concentrating, trying to pinpoint the source, identify the cause. It came from the centre of the shack – from *underneath* the shack – a gurgling, bubbling sound. 'Water! Dear God, I can hear water!' she whispered, shaking Ed Juan.

'Can you see it?' Evita stood in the darkness above Ed Juan, who was on his hands and knees with one ear to the shack floorboards.

'How can I see under the shack?' he said. 'I'll have to take the boards up. Pass me the shovel. And bring the lantern.'

Ed Juan wedged the steel spade between two of the boards and pushed down to lift old timbers. Then together they knelt beside the hole in the floor, gazing in wonder at the small fountain of water springing from the earth. 'It can't be, it is impossible!' Ed Juan reached down to touch it, feeling the coldness with his fingers.

'You are like the disciple Thomas,' Evita said as she watched Ed Juan scooping up the precious liquid in his cupped hand and gulping it down. 'Thomas did not believe Jesus had risen from the dead until he saw the nail marks in his hands and put his fingers where the nails were. I told you God would help us. It is a fountain from heaven, even though it rises from the desert.'

Ed Juan was crying, but his tears were lost among the drops of water splashing against his face. 'Thank you, God!' he breathed. 'Thank you!'

The spring was still bubbling and gurgling as they lay on the bed. 'Do you think it will stop soon?' Ed Juan asked, stroking his bloated stomach with one hand and smoothing his wet hair with the other.

'I don't know,' Evita answered. 'Maybe you should put the board back.' She looked toward the door. 'Are you sure you cannot see where it is coming from? Did you look behind the shack?'

'There is nothing,' Ed Juan said. 'There is no water running behind or in front of the shack. The chain is still on the pump and the earth around the well is dry. Outside you cannot hear the running water.' He sat up quickly and placed his hand on Evita's arm. 'We should fill the pails, and the flask, just in case it dries up.'

Evita gently pushed him back down. 'It won't dry up,' she said.

'But . . .' Ed Juan tried to sit up again. Evita placed her arm across his chest.

'Don't worry, God has provided this water and he won't take it away until we are ready to leave.'

'But what if John McCreery finds it?' Ed Juan said. 'He will think we have done something to the well.'

'Trust in God, Ed Juan. Don't doubt him.' Evita took a drink from a cup. 'Can't you see that God is taking care of things for us?'

When they awoke the spring had dried up. Ed Juan worried about it all day. He could not concentrate on his work. *What if there is no more fountain,* he thought, *and our lips crack and bleed again, and our mouths are dry and filled with dust while John McCreery drinks from his crystal glass?* But that night, soon after sundown, the water began to flow again. The next night, too, the spring brought water. And the next. Each night for a month the underground spring spouted from the desert, from sundown to sunrise.

John McCreery never found out. Ed Juan and Evita were careful to keep it a secret, although they were sure the old man suspected. 'Have you learned the secret of the kangaroo rat?' he asked when a week had passed. 'Maybe you're smarter than you look. Maybe you're stealing from the well and I don't know about it.' But he knew Ed Juan and Evita had not drawn water from the well, and he knew there was no water in the desert.

'God is sustaining us,' Evita told him, but the old man laughed, a mocking, raucous laugh.

'There are no Mexicans in heaven,' he taunted. 'For you there is only this desert hell. You will live and die here, right here on my ranch where *I* am God.'

'You are not God,' Evita said. 'God does not hurt people, he does not torture, he does not kill. He is the river of life. You should remember this, John McCreery.'

The old man shook his head. 'Stupid Mexicans,' he hissed. 'Get back to work. You can drink from the troughs tonight, if that is okay with God.' And he walked back to the house, laughing.

That night Ed Juan and Evita rode out into the desert in search of a new life. John McCreery stumbled across the ranch, drunk from whiskey, his throat dry as the red earth. He looked up at the stars and cursed the cloudless sky. He fumbled with the lock and chain and cursed again when he pumped the handle and no water came from the tap.

The well was dry.

3

Secret Cargo

RUSSIA, 1966

The Opel station wagon slowed down as it neared the border checkpoint. Rolf eased his foot off the accelerator and glanced at Elena sitting nervously beside him. She was looking through the windscreen at the six security officers who stood waiting for them. 'Start praying,' said Rolf. 'Start praying that God would confuse these men's thinking, and don't stop until they have finished their search and we are free to go.'

Rolf thought about the large cargo of Bibles hidden in the back of the vehicle and his heart rate quickened as they pulled up to the stop line. Smuggling of all kinds was on the increase and the guard at the Russian border had been trebled. The papers were full of stories of arrests, fines, imprisonment. The risk of being caught was great, but greater still was their determination to get these Bibles into the hands of Christians who had been deprived of God's Word.

The six security officers stood stone-faced as Rolf jumped out of the car and went around to hold the door for Elena. The guards approached the couple. One of the men held a piece of paper in his hand. He watched and listened as the young couple chatted casually about the unusual honeymoon they were having, visiting a number of East European countries.

'And I see this is not the first time either,' said the officer holding the paper. Rolf listened anxiously as the list of places he had visited on his last trip to Russia was read off. The officer added no comment, but Rolf was shaken. The guards moved quickly to search the station wagon. Two officers poked into every corner of the car on the inside, rifling through Rolf and Elena's belongings. Three others examined the outside: the engine, tyres, hub-caps. They rolled windows up and down to see if they stuck halfway, thumped the panelling, felt under wheel arches and sills.

One officer took no part in the inspection. He spent his entire time scrutinising the faces of Rolf and Elena. He was looking for the tell-tale signs of guilt: a nervous glance, a bead of perspiration – anything that would give the game away. and all the while the two secretly prayed: 'Confuse their thinking . . .'

The inspection seemed to last for hours. The guards would not give up, determined to find anything that was classified as contraband.

'Let me give you a hand,' said Rolf as one of the men struggled to take their camping tent out of the car. He volunteered to open the glove compartment, take out the spare tyre, lift the tops off the air and oil filters. It was a game of psychological war.

Then it was over. The guards had run out of places to search. The officer who had held the paper stepped forward. 'You were in Russia just a few weeks ago,' he said. 'Tell me, why is it that you take these frequent trips into our country?'

Rolf was leaning into the rear of the car, folding up the tent. He gave the canvas a slap. 'Well,' he said, 'my friend and I had such a wonderful time in your country that I decided to bring my bride here too. But there's another reason. We have a love for the Russian people. A special love.'

The officer stared at Rolf. He was not convinced, but his men had found nothing in the car, so he handed back Rolf's papers and reluctantly gave the order to open the barrier bar.

Rolf and Elena could hardly believe what had happened, and as they drove away from the border they laughed and wept with joy and relief. The guards had been within millimetres of the hundreds of Bibles stashed in the back. They were only amateurishly hidden. A thorough, determined search could hardly fail to discover them.

Unless . . .

4

The Dead-Zone

SAKHALIN ISLAND, PACIFIC OCEAN,
Russian Far East, May 1995

When the earthquake struck the lights went out on Pete Stein's world. He had been in bed reading when he had felt a slight tremor. Moments later the full force of the shock wave hit, blowing him across the room. His body struck the wall and searing pain shot through his head. Then nothing. He was unconscious when the rest of the apartment building collapsed like matchwood. By the time the roof hit the ground Stein was dead.

Four thousand miles away in Moscow, television pictures showed the grim scenes of devastation. Pete Stein's friend, John Ribbeck, watched in horror. He knew Pete was somewhere on Sakhalin, either in the island's capital, Yuzhno-Sakhalinsk, or maybe in the oil town of Neftegorsk, which had been flattened when the quake shook the north of the island at one minute past midnight local time. Almost the entire population of 3,200 had been asleep.

'The earthquake, measuring 7.5 on the Richter scale, is the most devastating in Russian history,' the television reported. 'There isn't a single wall standing in the entire town. Hope of finding survivors trapped under the rubble is fading. Temperatures are expected to fall to zero minus three tonight and will prove fatal to those buried alive. The number of dead could reach 2,500.'

Ribbeck slumped back into his chair. He felt sick. *Maybe Pete is okay*, he thought, remembering that Stein was not scheduled to arrive in Neftegorsk until next week. Stein and Ribbeck had worked together for two years. Both were exceptional photographers and had planned to travel to Sakhalin's northern port of Okha where they hoped to film tidal waves in the Sea of Okhotsk. But Stein ended up making the trip alone after Ribbeck accepted an offer of two weeks' work in Moscow instead. They had arranged to meet in Moscow later the following month before returning home to Cape Town in South Africa. Now Ribbeck wondered whether he would ever see Stein alive again. He closed his eyes and prayed.

Stein had celebrated his 30th birthday in Cape Town before leaving for Russia. Ribbeck was six years older but born on the same day. Ribbeck was married with two children, Stein had no family, although Ribbeck's parents treated him as if he was their own son. They were horrified when Ribbeck called on the telephone to break the news. 'How can we be sure he's okay?' they asked.

'We can't,' answered Ribbeck. 'They've found over 1,000 survivors but there's no way of finding out whether Pete is among them. I don't know where he was staying when the earthquake struck. He knows how to reach me in Moscow but maybe he can't get through. It must be chaos over there. We'll just have to sit tight and pray he's all right.'

Ribbeck and Stein were committed Christians, members of a charismatic church in Cape Town. Ribbeck's wife, Helena, organised a prayer rota of more than 100 church members. By rota they would pray non-stop until Pete was found safe. Ribbeck agreed it was a good idea. He was staying with Christian friends in Moscow. 'We will pray also,' he told Helena. 'We must trust in God for Pete's safety.'

On Sakhalin Island smoke rose from the rubble and merged

with the fog that drifted among the remains of apartment buildings. Throughout the night rescue workers searched for survivors beneath the glare of emergency floodlights. The numbing drone of rescue equipment mingled with the shouts of people calling out the names of missing relatives and friends. Then, every now and then, a calculated, expectant hush as rescue workers stopped and machinery shut down while everyone listened for any sound that would lead them to survivors under the rubble. Beneath the mounds of concrete blocks and twisted steel, people buried alive were still breathing, refusing to die as they lay trapped in complete darkness, unable to move, praying for help to arrive.

Peter Stein's lifeless body was wedged in a small, narrow hole between two concrete panels. Another man lay underneath him. This man was alive but couldn't move. His legs were pinned down and broken. In the darkness the man had reached out his hand and touched Stein's head. He prodded and pushed with his fingers. 'Are you alive? Are you alive?' he had asked. But there was no response. The man knew he was lying underneath a corpse.

As the search entered its third day more than 1,000 survivors had been found and almost 400 bodies pulled from the ruins. Bodies lay on the ground beneath blankets, and on the edge of town large graves were being dug.

They found Stein's body in the early hours of the morning, when the ground temperature had fallen to zero minus four and the dense fog had thrown a suffocating blanket over the desolation.

The man trapped underneath was unconscious, but rescue workers found a pulse and lifted him clear of the rubble. His legs were badly smashed but he was alive.

One of the rescue workers crawled down into the hole where Stein's body was wedged. He checked for signs of life but found none. 'He's dead,' the worker said simply. They lifted the corpse from between concrete panels and carried it to where twenty or thirty other bodies lay on the ground. A doctor checked Stein as the rescuers laid him to rest at the end of the line. The doctor shook his head and placed a blanket over the dead man.

Ribbeck was getting worried. It had been six days since the quake had struck and he was finding it impossible to get any news from Neftegorsk. The church in Cape Town had prayed continuously for five days and were still praying when Ribbeck received a call from the Russian daily newspaper, *Komsomolskaya Pravda*.

'Is that John Ribbeck?' a voice asked.

'Yes, speaking.'

'Mr Ribbeck, my name is Viktor. I am a reporter with *Komsomolskaya Pravda*. I have a message for you from Yuzhno-Sakhalinsk. Do you know where that is?'

'Yes. Yes, I do,' Ribbeck said, leaning against the wall for support. He felt his chest tighten.

'A colleague of mine has been talking to survivors of the earthquake. I believe he met a friend of yours at the hospital in Yuzhno-Sakhalinsk yesterday. He has no identification but says his name is Stein, Peter Stein. He remembered your name and address in Moscow, Mr Ribbeck. Do you know this man? Mr Ribbeck? Mr Ribbeck, are you still there?'

John Ribbeck was speechless. He could hear the voice at the other end but just stared blankly at the receiver. He was shaking. 'Yes, I know him,' he said. 'I thought he was dead. I thought we'd lost him.'

'No, he is alive,' the reporter confirmed. 'He is in a bad way but off the danger list. I will give you the telephone number of the hospital, Mr Ribbeck. I am not sure if you will get through just now but your friend is there. I am happy for you, Mr Ribbeck.'

Peter Stein had suffered terrible injuries, as Ribbeck discovered when he arrived at the hospital in Neftegorsk a few days later. 'His skull, cheekbone and nose were smashed. He also sustained serious crush injuries to his neck, shoulders and chest, and fractures to both arms and legs,' the doctor told Ribbeck. 'He is lucky to be alive – in fact one of the medics who found him swears he was dead. By all accounts they were getting ready to bury him.'

Ribbeck shuddered. 'Can I see him?'

'Yes, of course. He's through there,' said the doctor.

'He is still very weak but he has made excellent progress over the past week.'

Stein was awake. He started crying when his friend walked into the room. Ribbeck didn't know what to say. Tears filled his eyes. 'It's good to see you, Pete,' he said, and bent to kiss his friend's bandaged head. 'I thought you had gone to be with the Lord, buddy, but I guess the Big Man doesn't want you home yet. A lot of prayers went up for you, Pete – and God answered them.'

Stein smiled, 'I know, John. I saw all the people praying. I think I saw heaven too. I don't remember much about what happened, but I felt myself falling, slipping away, and then everything went black. I was real scared. It was cold and I couldn't see or feel. I wanted to scream but I was paralysed.'

Ribbeck grinned, so pleased to hear Stein's voice again.

'Then I felt myself floating, moving upwards out of the darkness. I couldn't stop it, I was just flying, man – flying through space. Then I stopped and could feel ground, something solid under my feet, but couldn't see where I was standing. There was light, blinding light, and I had to shield my eyes. I felt warmth radiate through my body and then I . . . I felt the presence of God. I know it was him, John, I just know it. I couldn't look into the light, it was like the sun only ten times brighter.'

Now Stein gave a big grin. 'I saw our church and people praying, and I looked down and saw my body lying on the ground with lots of other bodies covered in blankets. I started tingling all over – like pins and needles, and hot oil – but it felt good. And then it was over. It was dark again and cold and I was lying down with something over my face. I felt someone grab my arm and pain shot through my body. I heard a scream and this guy pulled a blanket off me and started shouting and waving his arms all over the place. The next thing I know I'm here in hospital. Do you think I'm crazy, man?'

John Ribbeck was kneeling by the bed, shaking his head. He started laughing and couldn't stop. He put his hands up to his face to wipe his tears away, and just laughed and laughed. Tears rolled down his cheeks and his body shook. He felt as if *he* was the one who'd received the greatest gift of all.

5

Deep Breathing

The man at the bottom of the sea had not long to live, and he knew it. He was trapped, foot wedged in razor-sharp coral, and his lungs were bursting. As he thrashed around, frantically trying to free himself, the crystal-clear water became clouded with crimson as blood seeped from lacerations. The pain he felt was numbed by the fear of dying, and yet a strange calm began to flood his mind.

Soon his mouth would be forced open as he gasped for air that he knew did not exist in this place. Then the ocean would consume him, filling his lungs ... choking ... suffocating ... drowning. This had always been the most terrifying thing he could imagine – the nightmare death he had always feared. But as he opened his mouth to scream, something happened to him, something that he may never fully understand. He started to breathe.

He was floating, his foot anchored to the ocean floor, like a balloon tethered to the ground. Light penetrated the surface thirty feet above. He could see the bottom of his boat, and a shoal of small fish passing beneath it. He looked down and saw the crimson cloud and felt the sharpness of the coral on his skin. He felt the pulse pounding in his head and tasted the saltness. But the ocean was not inside him, replacing the air he breathed.

He opened his mouth wider, feeling his jaw pop, and gulped.

No water entered his mouth. He was breathing normally, and as he floated he felt himself drifting away. He was still trapped but as he closed his eyes, shutting out blues and greens and rays of white light, the sensation of being carried, lifted gently, touched every fibre of his being.

The man's wife had sensed something was wrong. For hours now she'd felt uneasy, ever since her husband had left their hotel room and gone to the beach to hire a boat to row out on the calm blue ocean. He'd wanted to experience the solitude, the emptiness of the sea. He'd wanted to feel the morning sun on his back, and the coolness of the water on his skin. He had told his wife: 'I won't be back until late afternoon. I want to fish and swim and dive for shells.'

'Be careful,' she'd told him.

'Don't worry, I will,' he'd said, kissing her gently on the cheek.

Now she remembered that kiss as she sat on the edge of the bed holding a Bible and biting her lip. She was a devout Christian. He had lost his faith in God. 'Why? Because my father was a minister and both he and my mother died in a car crash,' he would tell people who asked why he did not share his wife's belief in God.

They were both in their forties, but she looked much younger, radiant, naturally beautiful and youthful. He could not deny it; his wife had changed since she'd become a Christian. She was a different woman, always happy, content, kinder, more sensuous. He knew it had something to do with God. And – he would never admit it – he was jealous.

She longed for him to share her faith, but loved him too much to try to pressure him. Besides, deep down she felt that he *wanted* to believe. He was just stubborn, proud, and she smiled as she sat on the bed remembering the kiss.

The uneasy feeling returned, like a wave to the shore, rolling in on her senses to worry her mind. She closed her eyes, clenched them shut, tight, trying to see light in the darkness. 'Oh, God,' she sighed, 'why am I feeling this way? Where have these troubled thoughts come from? Why am I so anxious?'

She breathed deeply, feeling a pain in her chest as she exhaled. 'God, if he's in some kind of trouble please keep him safe. Send your angels to watch over him.' Tears filled her eyes and she felt a strange burning ache within. 'I don't know what's going on, God, but I feel he needs you now, really needs you to be with him. Help him, save him. Thank you for hearing my prayer.'

Sun shone through the balcony doors and she stood up, opened them, and walked outside. It was a hot day but the sea breeze cooled the air. She stood for a while gazing out across the hotel grounds, raising a hand to shield her eyes from the glare. She saw whitecaps far out at sea and the sails of boats in the bay. She wondered where her husband was.

Out on the waves a rescue launch came alongside the husband's boat. 'She's empty,' the long-haired youth said, leaning over the side.

The bearded skipper nodded. 'Tie her up and we'll do a search. It could be just a drifter, but we'd better make sure.' The youth threw a small anchor into the ocean, climbed into the empty boat and tied it to the launch.

'Can you see anything?' The long-haired youth was watching the skipper leaning over the side of the boat, his face on the surface of the ocean as he looked through a glass mask. The water was crystal clear.

'Nothing,' he said. 'There's nothing down there.' He got up putting down the mask and running his fingers through his hair. 'Shall we do a quick dive?'

The long-haired youth glanced at his watch. 'All right. But if I'm late today she'll kill me.'

The bearded man laughed as they stripped down to their trunks. 'It's not deep here, so we'll try without the tanks first.'

They swam close to the level sea bed, looking around for a

corpse, but there was nothing down there. It was clear from where the bottom sloped toward the beach to the coral reef about two hundred yards away.

The bearded man came up first and gasped for air. 'I can't stay down as long as I used to,' he said when the long-haired youth surfaced. 'What was that – about three minutes?'

'Two,' said his colleague, smiling. 'You must be getting old. Let's swim out above the reef and try there, then we'll tow the boat back and beach it. Maybe someone will claim it later.'

They reached the reef – a favourite spot for divers – and could see the dark shapes of the coral distorted beneath the surface. 'I suppose the boat could have drifted in from here,' the bearded man said.

Under water the long-haired youth signalled to the bearded man to check the coral nearest to them before swimming off to look behind the reef. The bearded man found nothing and ran out of air before he could swim after the long-haired youth.

He gasped for air on the surface again, feeling the sun on his face. *I remember when I could stay down for four minutes,* he thought, rubbing his beard. *He doesn't even gasp when he comes up.*

But suddenly the long-haired youth broke through the surface, gasping, choking, his eyes wide. 'Down there, in the reef,' he spluttered. 'Down there, he's down . . .' He coughed and gasped for air again.

'Calm down, calm down,' the bearded man said. 'Deep breaths, come on, deep breaths. You've swallowed half the ocean.'

The youth grabbed hold of the skipper's shoulder. 'There's a dead man down there! He's trapped in the coral. Looks like his foot is caught.'

'Okay, okay. Let's get the gear. Are you all right to dive?'

'Yeah, I'm fine, it was just the shock. I saw him floating and opened my mouth. Thought I was going to end up like him.'

They swam back to the launch and pulled on oxygen tanks and

breathing masks. The bearded man put a large, broad-bladed knife in a leather tool holder and fastened it around his waist. 'Let's go,' he said.

He doesn't look dead, the long-haired youth thought as they swam closer to the figure floating in the middle of the reef.

He does look a bit weird, the bearded man thought, noticing the puzzled expression on his colleague's face. *His eyes are closed, like he's sleeping.* Most of the corpses he'd found at the bottom of the ocean had their eyes wide open – wide open with fear before they died.

The thought stayed with him and they approached the body. They both looked down at the coral where the man's foot was trapped. The bearded man felt around the swollen, lacerated ankle. The foot was caught in a narrow cleft, but after several minutes of hacking at the reef with the knife it was free and the body turned and floated horizontally.

The two men looked at each other before taking hold of an arm each and heading back to the surface with the body in between them. Back at the launch the bearded man climbed aboard first and it took all his strength to lift the body on board. It ended up face down on the deck. The long-haired youth grabbed the side of the boat but before he could pull himself in the bearded man let out a scream and jumped back as the 'drowned' man twitched and then coughed.

'I don't believe it! He's alive!' the skipper gasped, grabbing the youth's arm and pulling him into the boat. 'Quick, turn him over.'

The man's eyes were still closed but as he coughed again they blinked and opened. The bearded man's hand was shaking as he held the diver's head. The long-haired youth just knelt over the body with his mouth wide open. The man coughed again, louder this time, then spluttered and gasped and sat up quickly. The long-haired youth recoiled, almost falling overboard.

'Where am I?' the man croaked, looking at the long-haired youth. But he was speechless.

'We found you trapped under the water,' the bearded man answered. 'We thought you were dead.'

The diver looked at the ocean, then at his ankle, which was bleeding. 'Just a few cuts and bruises, that's all. Apart from that I feel fine.' His rescuers looked at each other, unable to believe what they'd seen.

The skipper was still shaking when he asked: 'Have you any idea how long you were down there?' He looked at his watch. 'It's three in the afternoon.'

The diver was holding his ankle now and closed his eyes to try to remember. 'It's all hazy,' he told them. 'Can't recall what happened.' Suddenly his eyes blinked open again, making the skipper jump. 'The stop watch,' he said. 'It's in the boat. I was timing my dives, to see how long I could stay down.'

The long-haired youth looked over the side and reached into the diver's boat. The watch's digital timer was still counting. It had passed the six-hour mark. The long-haired youth stared at the watch before handing it to his colleague. 'When did you start the timer?' he asked.

'Before the first dive,' came the reply.

'When did you get your foot caught?'

'On the first dive.' The man saw the shocked look on both faces and snatched the watch from the bearded man's hand. The display read six hours and three minutes. 'Oh my God, it can't be!' he said. 'I can't have been down there for six hours.'

The man's wife prayed all the way to the hospital. The skipper had called her at the hotel. 'Don't worry,' he told her, 'your husband's fine. He's had some kind of boating accident, that's all.'

When the doctor had finished his examination he told the diver: 'You've got a nasty gash on your ankle and your foot's in a bit of a mess, but otherwise you're fine.'

His wife thanked the doctor as she left the room and then sat on the edge of the bed and kissed her husband. 'I knew you were in trouble,' she said.

'I know, I saw you praying for me,' he told her. 'I thought I was going to die and then I must have fallen asleep and had a dream. I saw you sitting on the bed in the hotel room, praying. There were angels in the room with you, angels with wings.'

She grinned at him. 'I guess God wasn't taking any chances if he sent angels.'

He nodded thoughtfully. 'What I can't figure out is *why*. Why did he spare me? I mean, I should be dead. Why did he let me live?'

She squeezed his hand and smiled gently. 'I think you know the answer to that.'

He nodded. 'Yes, I think I do.'

6

'Faith and Destination'

TROPICAL DISEASE HOSPITAL,
somewhere in Scotland, 1982

The doctors had given up all hope of saving Father John Lochran. A priest in the prime of his life, he had been a missionary in Zaire for four years when he became very ill.

'I had spores in my lungs,' he recalls, 'which left me struggling for breath. I spent two years in hospital but they could not find out what was wrong. All they could do was give me heavy doses of cortisone to keep me alive.

'By the end of those two years the doctors had given up. Whatever was wrong with me, it was getting worse. I was in danger of going blind. And, to be honest, I too had given up hope. I was also very bitter against God. I felt my years in Africa had been a waste of time, and I was just waiting for the end.'

But at that point, when the hospital chaplain thought it wouldn't be long before he read John the last rites, a Catholic sister told him he ought to go to Lourdes.

'I knew many wonderful healings had taken place in that pilgrimage town,' he says, 'but I was very sick and really couldn't face travelling to France. But then the sister sent me a ticket, so I thought I'd better make the effort. My faith was at an all-time low by then, but there was a flicker of hope that made me wonder if God had prompted her to send that ticket. If so – and it was pretty clear that only God could do anything for me – I had to grasp the opportunity.'

John spent almost a month in Lourdes, hoping, praying, but his condition remained severe, to the point that he could hardly walk.

'Then, a few days before I was due to leave, I had what I can only describe as a healing sensation. There were no flashing lights but, quite suddenly, I was completely better. I stopped taking cortisone the very next day, and when I went back to the hospital, they did some X-rays and told me the disease had just burnt itself out.

'My family couldn't believe it. It certainly did not happen because I was a pious man. The fact is, I was disillusioned and angry. But afterwards I felt that, if I remained healthy, I would like to help other people who were in a similar state. I was given the opportunity to do just that when, later on, I was invited back to Lourdes as chaplain to the English-speaking pilgrims.'

7

The Boy and the Beast

NORTHERN ALBERTA, CANADA, JANUARY 1990

Eleven-year-old Daniel Olin was lost in the mountains, and fear, as well as night, was closing in on him. Hours earlier he had thrown some provisions into his school rucksack and run away from home. Now the shadowy shapes and scary sounds of the Canadian wilderness were getting to him, and he ached to be home. The pain in his badly smashed ankle was getting worse, and it was getting colder too. He could not have felt more miserable. Or more afraid.

He lay on the ground, exhausted, and tried to remember how he had got here. Not just the route he'd taken into the outback, but the unhappy sequence of events that had led him to leave home and travel almost 400 kilometres from Edmonton to the Rocky Mountain town of Jasper. It was all such a blur now. It had been less than twenty-four hours since he had posted that note to his father on the refrigerator and walked out by the back door, but to Daniel it felt like forever. He thought there was no way back and started to cry.

The creature, crouching in the darkness beneath the branches of a large spruce, thrust its ears forward, straining to the strange sounds from the slope above. The flash of its burning amber eyes and brilliant-white muzzle pierced the gathering darkness, its only thought the thicket where the boy lay shivering in the snow. His faint whimpering carried on the chill mountain air and something stirred deep within the creature. Its muscles tensed, its tail beat and swept the ground. And then it moved, quickly; a single, arching bound, twenty feet across the slope, ascending the rocks toward the boy.

The Olins had moved from Washington DC in the summer of 1987. John Olin, an accountant, had been made redundant two days before Thanksgiving the previous year and could not afford to turn down the offer of a job with a finance company in Edmonton, Alberta. John's wife Ruth, whose parents and sister lived in Washington, was not keen to move north, but they had bills to pay.

Ruth's apprehension about the move was fuelled by comments from her brother, Jack, who pastored a church near Vancouver. He told his sister she would not like Edmonton. 'It's a different world up here,' he said. 'Folks can just kinda lose themselves.'

Daniel, an only child, was eight and hated the idea of moving. His parents had tried to reassure him, but the boy was afraid of the unknown, of starting a new school and having to make new friends. As the moving date drew near he became angry and resentful.

They rented a house on the outskirts of the city, a stone's throw from the North Saskatchewan River. John settled into his new job, Ruth started working part-time as a motel receptionist downtown, and Daniel found he liked his new school, where he became popular as the boy who used to live across the street from the President of the United States. 'We weren't that close to the White House,' he'd tell them, but it didn't matter anyway. The new kid on the block was making friends, and after a while Edmonton didn't seem such a bad place to live. Even the bitter winters that ravage Alberta's capital, one of Canada's most north-erly cities, failed to dampen his enthusiasm. The Olins were adjusting to a new way of life, and it looked as though everything was going to work out fine. But that was before Harry walked into their lives.

Harry ran his own haulage truck out of Edmonton, usually down Highway 16, the Yellowhead Highway, to the Rocky Mountain national parks. Sometimes he'd take a load from the city up to Yellowknife in the North West Territories, or down to Calgary and Medicine Hat, before riding the Trans-Canada Highway to Regina and Winnipeg. He would be gone for days, sometimes a week or more, before returning to the motel, where he'd kept a room for two years. It was there he met Ruth, and there the affair began. It lasted three months and Ruth ended up moving out of the house. She took a room at the motel the day after she had told John about the affair. 'It was a big mistake and it's over,' she said, 'but I can't live here any more so I'm moving out. I guess things were not right between us anyway. It's my fault, I'm sorry.'

John was shocked. 'I know our marriage is not perfect, but it's too good to throw away,' he told her. 'If you need time out, that's okay, stay at the motel for a while. I'm here for you, we're both here for you. And don't worry about Daniel; he'll be fine.'

But Daniel was far from fine. His world had been torn apart and he was afraid. John did his best to hold things together, but he was working long days and drinking too much at night. Every day he'd ask, 'How are you doing, son? Hanging in there?'

Daniel would say, 'I guess so,' but he was just putting on a brave face. Ruth would meet him from school most days and they'd go back to the motel and swim in the pool or watch cable TV.

Frequently he asked, 'When are you coming home, Mum?' But Ruth would just shrug her shoulders and say, 'I'm not sure, honey. Why, are you missing me?' Daniel would nod, and he'd get a big hug and kiss, and they both would cry. Ruth would tell him,

'You're the best, Danny, and I'll always love you, you know that.'
But Daniel didn't know for sure. He wasn't sure about anything
any more. So he ran away. He wrote a note which he stuck to the
refrigerator door. It read: Dad, I don't think Mum's ever gonna
come home. You're going to get divorced just like Billy Johnson's
mum and dad and he ended up living in a home. I'm not gonna
do that so I'm going live with Uncle Jack instead. I love you both.
Danny.

He stuffed a handful of clothes, three candy bars, his walkman,
and a map of Canada into his school rucksack. He took thirty
dollars from his dad's wallet and slipped quietly out of the back
door. It was five-thirty on Friday morning and freezing cold. John
Olin was sleeping off the previous night's whiskey and would not
have woken even if Daniel had slammed the back door. *He won't
be up for another few hours*, Daniel thought. *Guess he'll just think I've
gone to school early*.

Daniel knew he had to head downtown for Jasper Avenue and
then out to the Yellowhead Highway where he thought he would
be able to hitch a ride from one of the truck stops. He wasn't sure
exactly how far Vancouver was but he guessed that it could not
be more than three or four days' ride. His plan was to thumb a lift
down the Yellowhead to Jasper townsite at the foot of the Rocky
Mountains, around 350 kilometres west of Edmonton. From
Jasper, he would hitch a ride across the Rockies to Vancouver. It
looked pretty straightforward on the map.

There wasn't much moving out of the truckstop, and Daniel
thought he would freeze to death as he walked around the parking
lot searching for a ride. The temperature had dropped to ten
below in the night and even though Daniel had pulled on several
layers he was shivering.

He stood by the roadside, underneath a giant Exon sign,
wondering whether his plan was such a good idea. A silver truck
started to pull off the gas station behind him and Daniel ran across

the lot and on to the other side of the slip road. The truck disappeared behind the gas station house and Daniel heard the engine rumble into a lower gear before the road panned out and dropped toward the highway.

The truck came into view again and Daniel quickly made for the middle of the first bend on the exit-way. He knew the truck would slow right down for the turn and stood there waving his arms. But the driver had no intention of stopping and sounded his horn. Daniel stood rooted to the spot.

'What the hell . . .' roared the driver, and slammed on the brakes. The truck rolled to a stop next to Daniel and the driver leaned out of the window. 'What the hell are you trying to do, kid, get yourself killed?'

They'd been driving for two hours when Harry found out who Daniel was. The colour just drained out of him. He spun the truck off the road and brought it screeching to a stop on the hard shoulder. Daniel backed up against the door. 'What are you doing?' he asked. 'Why are we stopping?'

Harry slumped onto the steering wheel and clamped his hands on his head. 'This is not happening to me,' he muttered. 'It must be some kind of joke.' He turned to the boy. 'Has Ruth put you up to this? Did she send you looking for me? Come on, kid, talk to me, tell me there's some mistake. You ain't really Ruth Olin's boy, are you?'

Daniel nodded. 'Ruth is my mum's name. Do you know my mum? Does my mum know you?' The boy frowned. He was confused and a little frightened.

'Small world, eh, kid? Small world.' Harry smiled at Daniel. 'Did Ruth never mention me?'

'I don't know your name.'

'It's Harry.' He looked at Daniel for a reaction, for a change in the boy's face, but there was none.

'So you're gonna visit your uncle in Vancouver, eh?' Harry

raised his eyebrows. 'How come your folks didn't put you on the train or bus?' He shifted the gearstick and steered the truck back on to the highway. The boy clearly didn't know about him and Ruth. *It's just a stroke of luck, or bad luck, that he ended up hitching a ride with me*, he thought, *But that suits me fine.*

'How far to Jasper?' Daniel asked, looking out of the window.

'You haven't answered my question, kid. Do your folks know you're taking a ride out of town, or are you on the run?'

'I've left home. I wrote my dad a note but I didn't tell my mum, although I guess she'll find out soon enough. She was supposed to be meeting me from school today.'

Harry scratched his head. 'Kid,' he said in a loud, authoritative voice, 'at the next gas station you are gonna phone home and let 'em know just where you are. I ain't getting involved in no runaway situation. They'll be saying I kidnapped you or something like that. We'll get a message to Ruth and let her know that I'm bringing you home just as soon as we lose this load. Understand?'

Daniel continued to stare out of the window.

'Well, that's how it's gonna be,' Harry said. 'That's how it's gonna be.'

The escape plan was already forming in the boy's mind.

Harry stood at a payphone beside the highway, looking out over a valley while he waited for someone to answer his call. It had started to snow. Daniel sat in the truck, parked off the deserted road. In the summer this stretch would be jammed with cars bringing holiday-makers to climb in the Rocky Mountain foot-hills. But few folks set eyes on these slopes in the winter. Harry shivered and turned to look at the truck. The boy was looking back at him. *Crazy kid.*

The motel picked up and the receptionist fetched Ruth. 'What do you want, Harry?' she snapped.

Harry was about to tell her when out of the corner of his eye he saw Daniel jump from the truck. 'Hey, kid, stop!' he yelled, dropping the receiver. He ran after the boy but lost sight of him when he raced off the road and into the cover of spruce trees screening a rest area. Harry tried to cut him off by climbing the road wall but the slope on the other side was too steep and the snow made it impossible to grip. *Damn*. He stood on the wall and tried to spot the boy but there was no sign.

By the time he returned to the payphone Ruth had hung up. The second time he called she wouldn't come to the phone so he had to tell the receptionist what had happened. Ruth was breathless when she picked up. Harry repeated the story and Ruth became almost hysterical. 'Calm down, calm down,' Harry urged. 'Everything is going to be okay. He won't get far.'

Ruth was crying. 'It's all my fault, I've made him run away from home. If anything happens to him . . .'

'Hey, don't talk stupid; nothing bad is going to happen to him. Listen, someone up there must have his eye on Danny because the chances of him hitching a ride with me were slim. Think about it. He could have ended up with anybody – maybe with some crazy-head. But he didn't, he got me – and before you know it he'll be back home.'

Ruth was calmer now. 'Are you going after him, Harry? You mustn't let him get lost.'

The trucker scanned the valley. 'I can't see him; he must be in the woods down there. I'll have another look and then phone the sheriff. You'd better phone your brother in Vancouver. Let him know what Danny's up to.'

Ruth gasped. 'What! You don't think he'll make it that far? He couldn't, could he?'

Harry wished he'd never mentioned Vancouver. 'Ruth, let me tell you something, let me try to put your mind at ease. It's about two miles to the town of Jasper from here and I know that if Danny doesn't come back to the truck he'll get back on the road and head for town. If the sheriff doesn't pick him up first I'll bet my last dime I pass him on the road. As soon as I do I'll get him to call you.'

When Daniel headed into the forest he had no idea of where he was or where he was going. He just wanted to get far away from Harry, far away from Edmonton. Somehow, some way, he had to make it to Vancouver. *Uncle Jack will understand*, he thought. *He won't send me back home*. He could only see the top of the truck now, its exhaust stack poking above the road wall. Harry was calling his name, but he couldn't see him. The land had dropped sharply below the road and Daniel was running, following a stream bed through a tract of meadows and open woods. The snow and dry leaves crunched under his shoes, while overhead storm clouds gathered, smothering a pale winter sun.

The boy laboured up the steep cutlines, his legs aching and leaden. He stopped often to check his bearings, sometimes looking back, half hoping to see Harry. What he saw was a bleak landscape – a cruel, cold world that seemed to go on for ever. He headed for the foothills. Somewhere above him the Rockies were swathed in a rolling mist. Somewhere ahead of him the beast stirred in its lair.

Daniel was growing tired. An hour, maybe two hours, had passed now and his kneecaps burned as he ran headlong into another valley, the dense underbrush sapping his strength.

But he forced himself on, a mental picture of his Uncle Jack's house coming to his rescue each time he stumbled over a fallen tree or slipped on a snow-covered slope. That house was actually a thousand miles away, but Daniel was running as though it stood in the next valley. He made it to the top of the next foothill but the cutline down the other side was steeper than any he'd encountered before and it took him by surprise. He grabbed the branch of a spruce tree, trying to slow his pace, but he slipped and fell sideways. A snowdrift broke his fall but on the way down he caught his ankle on an outcrop of rock. Searing pain shot through his leg. The impact had smashed the bone.

Jack was on his knees, praying. Ruth had called. She'd told him the whole story and Jack could sense his sister was scared. Now he was talking to the 'Big Fella', as he called his God. 'I'm going to get on my knees and ask him to watch out for young Daniel,' Jack said. 'He knows exactly where he is and *will* protect him. But *you* must pray too, Ruth. You must place your trust in God. He won't let you down.'

In his study in Vancouver Pastor Jack replaced the receiver and got down on his knees. 'God, I ask you to keep Daniel from harm,' he prayed. 'Keep him safe right now.' He spoke softly, his head cradled in his hands, his elbows resting on his desk. 'Wherever he is, God, send your angels to protect him, and watch over him until he's found safe and sound.' He took a deep breath and looked up to heaven, as though the ceiling wasn't there. 'We need a miracle, Lord,' he said. 'Save that boy from freezing to death.'

The sheriff threw a thick thermal coat at Harry. 'Put it on,' he said, 'the temperature's dropping like a lead balloon.'

The two men stood by the payphone and looked out across the valley. 'Do you think we'll find him?' asked the trucker. 'How much light have we got left?'

'About an hour.' The sheriff handed him a flashlight. 'If we're lucky the kid won't have got far. We've got a car doing the rounds in town and checking the roads again. Maybe he'll show up. If he does they'll get us on the radio; if not, we'll keep looking till we find him.'

'How far do you reckon he's got?'

'It's hard to say,' said the sheriff. 'Eleven-year-old kid, out here . . . who knows? It's pretty tough going out there, especially in this weather. I reckon two miles at the most. If he's out there, he'll more than likely be holed up in some cave. You said you reckon he's got food?'

Harry nodded. 'I think he's got some supplies in his sack, but I'm not sure. I don't think he figured on going hiking. Crazy kid . . .'

The sheriff and Harry climbed the grey-stone road wall and headed down into the underbush, following a stream bed through the valley meadow. They hadn't got a clue which way the boy had gone. 'Don't look for footprints,' the sheriff told Harry, 'you won't find any. Snow's been falling heavy for hours now. Just keep hollering his name and pray for luck.'

The two men trudged through the deep white carpet, halting every few minutes to call out, their shouts shattering the silence for a moment, then hopelessly lost in the depths of the descending winter night. They didn't know it, but they were heading in the right direction, actually following the same path Daniel had taken hours earlier. It was almost as though they were being drawn to where the boy lay.

Daniel had become hypothermic. He lay on the frozen ground, his whimpering silenced as he drifted in an icy sea of numbness. He didn't hear or see the mountain lion until it was upon him. It was a big male, maybe 150 pounds or more; a powerful, steely blue-grey cougar. It lay across the boy, its heavily muscled forelimbs across his chest and shoulders. Daniel felt the cougar's warm breath on his face. He couldn't move, but he was not paralysed by fear. His senses were deadened by the shock of the cold and pain, but he could still feel the animal's pulse beating against his own, and he was not afraid.

The cougar lay across the boy, silently, without menace. From time to time it nuzzled Daniel, pressing its face into his neck, licking snow from his skin, radiating body heat. Daniel felt the animal's warmth seep through and wanted to lift his arms to draw the animal closer, to pull it tighter and squeeze out the deathly chill. The cougar had its eyes closed. It was breathing deep and slow, the rhythm soothing. Daniel closed his eyes. He felt safe.

Somewhere, far away, as though in a distant dream, someone was calling his name.

Harry and the sheriff reached the small mountain where boy and cougar lay as one in the snow. They climbed the narrow cutline and stood at the top, not far from the thicket of spruce where their search would end. 'Danny, can you hear me?'

The cougar flinched, opening its eyes but staying low over the boy. It turned its head to face the two men head on, its big round eyes fixed on them. The boy was sleeping. He was perfectly at peace.

Harry shouted again, walking across the steep cutline where Daniel had fallen. He looked down, spotted the cougar, and froze. The sheriff was right behind him.

'Don't move, just stay right there, don't move a muscle.' The sheriff reached down for his gun. He didn't take his eyes off the cougar. The big cat stared back, as still as a statue, snow glistening in a ridge across its neck and back.

Harry could feel his heart hammering in overdrive. His mouth was dry, chest tight as a tourniquet. 'Is he dead? I can't tell,' he whispered.

The sheriff, gun in one hand, raised the other slowly to signal Harry to calm down. But suddenly Daniel woke and lifted his head off the ground. The cougar sat up, one paw still across the boy's chest.

Harry screamed: 'Shoot! Shoot it!' But the sheriff fumbled and the gun fell barrel first into the snow. The cougar bent forward, lowering its head towards Daniel's face. It licked the boy's forehead and, before the sheriff had time to pick up the gun, turned around and disappeared into the thicket and down the other side of the mountain.

Harry ran over to Daniel. 'Don't move, kid,' he said. 'Are you hurt bad? Can you speak?'

Daniel sat up. 'I'm fine, it's just my ankle.' He looked up at the sheriff. 'You were going to shoot him, weren't you?'

'Damn right I was,' said the sheriff, 'and if he comes back I'll blow him back down the other side of the mountain.'

'But he saved my life.'

The sheriff wasn't listening. He was watching Harry examine the boy. 'Is he cut bad? Is he badly mauled?'

'You're not going to believe this, but he ain't got a mark on him,' Harry said. 'His ankle looks broken, but the rest of him seems okay.'

'Must have showed up just in time,' the sheriff said. 'A minute later and you'd have been cougar food, kid.'

Daniel frowned. 'He was with me for hours, stopped me from freezing to death. He didn't want to hurt me.'

Harry looked at Daniel and then at the sheriff. The two men shook their heads in disbelief.

Daniel sat next to his Uncle Jack on the lounge sofa. The boy wore a plaster cast on his ankle. They were in the front room of John and Ruth Olin's house in Edmonton. A week had passed since the incident on the mountain.

'That was the sheriff on the phone,' John said, stepping into the room. 'Just wanted to make sure Daniel's okay.'

'That's nice of him,' said Ruth. She was standing behind the sofa, stroking Daniel's head. 'Did he say anything about the cougar?'

John looked confused. 'Yeah, he spoke to someone from the park ranger's department yesterday. He told them what happened down there; they didn't believe him, though. Told him he must have been seeing things.' John cleared his throat. 'They say a cougar would have killed Daniel, period. They said something about a cougar making its living from killing moose calves three times its size.'

'But this cougar was different, eh, Danny?' Jack squeezed the boy's shoulder. 'God sent this one to stop you from freezing to death up on that mountain. We know that, don't we?'

Daniel looked at his dad and reached behind to squeeze his mum's arm. 'Uncle Jack told me he asked God to protect me, and the sheriff said it was a miracle the cold didn't kill me. Even the doctor who examined me at the hospital said he couldn't believe it.'

'That's right,' said Jack, looking at John. 'They reckon it must have been at least minus fifteen up on that mountain. But he was as warm as toast when they found him.'

'I'm not doubting what happened,' John said. 'I thank God he's okay; it's just hard to believe, that's all. I talked to the doctor and the sheriff and they both reckon Daniel is lucky to be alive. The sheriff said the cougar should have killed him, even if the cold didn't. Poor guy, he sounded more confused than I am.'

'God answers prayers, John. The Big Fella really saved Daniel.' Jack laughed. 'After all, he created man and beast, and ain't that the truth.'

'Ruth, is that you?' Harry couldn't quite make out the whispered voice at the other end of the line.

'Yes, it's me, I've been expecting you to call.'

'How are you? How's Danny?' Harry felt uneasy, considering all that had passed between them.

'We're both fine,' Ruth answered. 'In fact we are *all* fine. John wants to thank you for what you did. We are back together now; we are a family again.'

'I'm glad, I'm pleased for you all. Sometimes it takes something like this to make you realise what's important in your life.' Harry paused. 'Ruth, look . . . your brother Jack called me last week. I guess he got my number off you?'

'Yes, he wanted to . . .'

'No, you don't have to explain, it's okay. He told me you and John were back together and that you've started going to church and all that. He said something about losing faith in God and finding it again. Well, he's invited me to his church in Vancouver.

'He reckons the same God that sent that cougar to save Danny can work a miracle in *my* life. I ain't completely sure what he means but I'm gonna give it a shot anyway. Listen, look after that kid. He's a bit special, Ruth, a bit special.'

8

In the Twinkling of an Eye

RALEIGH, NORTH CAROLINA, JUNE 1995

Elizabeth Jernigan was enjoying her birthday. She was twelve and it felt good. Her parents, Betsy and Leonard, had organised a swimming party and thrilled at the way Elizabeth and her friends splashed around in the lake next to their home. *I'm so proud of you, Elizabeth*, Betsy thought. *You are such a beautiful child, and so smart. You haven't missed a beat and the miracle keeps going on.*

Elizabeth was so happy she thought she would burst. Her face radiated joy, and it did not matter that her right eye was permanently closed. Elizabeth Jernigan could see enough of the beauty of life out of her good eye, and the view was resplendent.

There was a time when Betsy and Leonard Jernigan Jr believed Elizabeth would die. It was before the miracle and after the darkest hour. The time when hope is drained. The time when you can't feel for the fear in your life, or see for the fog in your mind.

Sometimes you pray for a way out but find none, listen for an answer but hear only an echo. It's then that faith is tested to the limit and your soul cries out for reason. Elizabeth was dying and Betsy and Leonard were preparing to let her go.

One day when baby Elizabeth was four months old her right eyelid began to weaken a little; the pupil seemed slow to respond to light. Betsy and Leonard were worried, but their child seemed happy and healthy, so they believed the problem would clear up by itself. It didn't.

Soon the eye began to droop and the pupil became fixed. The baby's grandfather, Isaac Manly, a Harvard trained surgeon, was worried about the child's symptoms. He suggested a trip to the ophthalmologist, which led to the paediatrician, then the neurologist. A brain tumour was diagnosed.

For five days Betsy and Leonard prayed for their daughter. 'We were both very scared, but prayed with a passion uncommon to both of us,' recalls Elizabeth's father, an attorney. The parents agreed to exploratory surgery, which carried a one-in-five chance of leaving Elizabeth permanently brain damaged.

Surgeons removed part of the tumour from the nerve that controls the movement of the right eye. Trying to get at the rest was too dangerous. But when they had finished and the pathology reports came back, the news could not possibly have been worse.

Elizabeth was suffering from an extremely rare malignant meningioma, which, according to the records, has killed everyone who ever had it. Her prognosis: continued growth of the aggressive tumour, grievous paralysis and certain death.

Betsy and Leonard were devastated, but they believed their daughter would be healed if it were God's will. They continued to pray; their friends prayed; their church prayed; Elizabeth's grandfather prayed, though he admits: 'I did not have the faith to pray for healing of this known malignancy. I prayed for guidance that we be led to the right doctors.'

But things went from bad to worse. Fluid began accumulating on Elizabeth's brain; doctors had to keep relieving the pressure. They said she would need more surgery to insert shunts that would drain the fluid. Hope was running out.

Elizabeth's grandmother was still believing for a miracle. She and her husband Isaac had invited a family friend – an Episcopal priest – to stay at their house over the weekend before the surgery.

After dinner on Sunday night, the grandparents asked the priest if he would anoint Elizabeth with consecrated oil while the family prayed. He did, and he left the oil for Betsy to use again and again during the next 48 hours until surgery. The praying continued.

The night before the scheduled shunt surgery a doctor arrived in Elizabeth's hospital room and removed so much thick, infected fluid from her brain that he asked to postpone the operation for a few days. But twelve hours later, when he returned to do another tap, he could barely find any fluid; the little he removed was totally clear. The doctor was confused. Elizabeth was back home two days later.

A month after the first operation the same surgeons made a final attempt to remove the rest of the tumour. But when they went into Elizabeth's brain they could not find the lesion. They removed a section of the nerve that the cancer had attacked, knowing that it would leave her blind in her right eye but agreeing that it represented her best hope of survival.

When the tissue was examined the pathologist could not find any cancer. Regular CAT scans since then have revealed no evidence of a tumour. One of the surgeons who operated on Elizabeth described what happened as 'spontaneous resolution'. Betsy and Leonard have another word for it.

9

Blind Eyes and Broken Backs

WEST TEXAS, SUMMER 1994

Joseph Spears stood and watched the landscape stretch in an unbroken line. The sunset was awe-inspiring and he breathed in the clear, dry air as the sky blazed with yellows, oranges and reds before fading to soft purple and pink as darkness descended.

Spears gazed at the heavens and marvelled at the beauty of creation. He felt dusk bring the cool breeze and tasted the chill of night. Then he saw the lights of many small towns in all directions, and above him the shining stars.

He saw different shades of darkness and remembered when he could see only one. The blackness that had consumed him for twenty-nine years had gone, his blind eyes opened, and he wanted to take in every particle of light, touch every vibrant colour. Spears could see and he lifted his arms toward the sky and thanked God.

They say truth is stranger than fiction, but Spears insists there is nothing unusual about his story. 'I'm just one of many who God has led to Medjugorje and healed,' he says. 'There ain't nothing mysterious or weird about it; the good Lord gives sight to the blind today, just like he did in the New Testament.'

Spears was born blind in both eyes but his friend Tom McPherson led him to the 'miracle town' of Medjugorje in the spring of '94 and his sight was fully restored. 'There is no medical explanation for it,' McPherson says. 'God simply worked a miracle in Joseph's life, just like he did for me two years earlier.'

McPherson, a tough-looking, leather-skinned 48-year-old Texan, broke his back riding a bull named Wild Cherry in the fall of 1974. 'I was one mean rodeo cowboy who feared neither God nor man,' he says, 'but the accident broke my body and my spirit. I became a cripple who could hardly walk and hated life until the Lord healed me near the summit of the Hill of Apparitions. It was incredible. God just kinda reached down and took all my pain away.'

The Hill of Apparitions climbs above the small Croatian town of Medjugorje. It's the place where six children claimed to have seen a heavenly vision in June 1981. Spears and McPherson are just two of eleven million people from all over the world who have visited Medjugorje in search of miracles.

Spears, like McPherson, was raised a Catholic, but to begin with was a little sceptical. 'I knew Tom before he was healed; afterwards I returned to my faith because I believed God had performed a great miracle. I mean, at first I couldn't see what had happened but people kept telling me how straight his back was and how he was running around all over the place and riding again.

'Tom's wife heard about the visions in Medjugorje and per-suaded Tom to go. He didn't even believe in God then, but he does now. When he told me that I should go so that God could restore my sight, I wasn't sure. I was born blind and didn't know any different, and I wasn't unhappy with my life, you know what I mean? I'd kinda got used to things the way they were. It was kinda like, "Hey, God made me this way, and he must've done it for a reason, so back off." I can sing and play the guitar real well, which is a gift from God, so I don't reckon he left me out at all.

'But anyway, everyone was excited about Tom's healing – me too, I guess – so I agreed to go. I just kinda said to God and to

Tom, "Well, if my eyes open, praise the Lord; if they don't, tough." I didn't build my hopes up; I wasn't that kind of guy. So we arrived at this little town, a Texan cowboy and a blind country-and-western singer, fresh from the wild west. I hadn't got a clue what the place looked like. In my mind I'd formed a picture of a beautiful walled city with a cathedral and ancient ruins.

'But Tom was giving me this running commentary as we walked; it was like, "Well, we're in the main street, Joe, the *only* street, Joe. There's a real ugly-looking church thing, and shops and restaurants. It's pretty modern, Joe, real ordinary." I was thinking, "Man, are you sure we're in the right place? Are you sure we ain't in downtown Amarillo or somewhere?" It didn't feel much like miracle city.

'But we found this little guesthouse place, and we ate and then Tom prayed for me. I didn't feel anything, maybe a little emotional after travelling half way around the world to see if God would take away my blindness. Tom went out hoping to catch a glimpse of the heavenly vision. I went to sleep; I was worn out, man. The furthest I'd ever been before was up to Kansas City to visit a relative.

'I guess I must have been asleep for a couple of hours or so when Tom came back. He was real excited. I asked him if he'd seen the vision. He hadn't, but he'd been talking to this woman who says she sees it every other day, and she'd told Tom to expect a great miracle. She said something about him being anointed or something. Anyway, Tom had asked this priest to come along, and they prayed with me. The priest laid his hand on my head and it happened.

'I felt warmth flooding my whole body; it was like getting under a hot shower, only it felt like I'd got warm oil running inside me as well. My head started feeling real strange, a tingling sensation, like pins and needles. It got more intense and then I felt someone rub something over my eyes, like oil, only the priest had both his hands on my head and I could feel Tom's hand on my back.

'I got scared for a moment, but then the tingling sensation spread all over my body and I started laughing; couldn't stop until these tiny little rays of light started appearing in my head. Up until then I'd kept my eyes closed, but right then I had to open them. I did, and it wasn't dark any more; there was blinding light and shapes that were not so bright.

'I tried to turn my head away from where the light was coming from but it was all around me. I got scared again, real frightened, but something inside me kept saying, "Fear not, God is with you," so I just lifted up my hands and started to praise the Lord. I think even the priest was surprised.'

Spears' blind eyes opened gradually. It took more than one day, but by the time they were ready to leave he was taking photographs of Medjugorje with McPherson's Nikon camera.

'I can't describe what it was like,' Spears says. 'I had been blind since birth. I had never seen my own face, the sky, the earth, nothing. It was like being born again.

'All the way home on the plane Tom kept saying, "Joe, quit staring, you're scaring folk." I just kept crying and laughing. I didn't want to close my eyes at all. I kept thinking maybe something's gonna go wrong any second now and the miracle's gonna wear off. But in my heart I knew it was for keeps.'

10

After the Fall

UNITED STATES OF AMERICA, JULY 1991

This is the story of two almost identical accidents and two amazing, identical miracles. They happened to young men of similar age, and both took place in the same country, in the same month of the same year.

Jason Hailey and Bobby Mescalaro were as good as dead. They were comatose and hooked up to life-support systems after suffering horrific injuries. Their respective surgeons were adamant that Jason and Bobby had no chance of recovery. Both sets of parents were trying to come to terms with their imminent loss. In each case neurologists were ready to disconnect the two broken bodies from hospital machinery. There was no hope, or so it was thought.

Hailey, a gifted 20-year-old athlete and scholar, had been on a family vacation back to Oklahoma, where he was a decorated student at Hobart High School before his family moved to Lakeland, Florida. It was three days after the Fourth of July and Jason was letting off fireworks with friends on an old country bridge. Turning quickly, he accidentally stepped off the edge. His body fell thirty feet, bounced off a tree limb and smashed head-first into the rocks of a dry creek-bed.

Jason's right eye socket was crushed, leaving a skull bone protruding into his brain. One lung collapsed. His heart was shifted by the impact. Emergency skull surgery was performed that night by the neurologist on call. He had seen it all before but was moved to tears by the extent of the damage he found. On his post-op report the surgeon wrote: 'I just operated on a young man who won't make it. It's too bad – he's only young and a fine athlete.' Jason lapsed into a coma. The trauma had caused his brain to swell.

Michael Hailey, pastor of First Baptist Church in Lakeland, and his wife Sandra prepared themselves for the inevitable. Their son was facing certain death. Neurologists at Oklahoma City hospital had outlined the option of shutting down Jason's life-support system. They were convinced it was the best thing to do.

But Michael Hailey kept on praying. Hour after hour, day after day, he lifted his comatose son in prayer to God. Something inside him kept believing for a miracle. And then it happened. Eight days after his accident, Jason's grandparents walked into his hospital room to find him sitting up, drinking orange juice. Within minutes Michael and Sandra Hailey were embracing their son, crying tears of unbridled joy.

Jason says he does not remember anything between stopping for gas near the bridge just before the fall and waking up in hospital. Medics could not take in the sight of the boy sitting up in bed. The neurologist who performed emergency skull surgery on him could offer no medical explanation. 'Something remarkable has taken place here,' he said afterwards. 'If I had not seen it with my own eyes I would not believe it.'

Within two days Jason was out of intensive care; in another week he was back at his Lakeland home. Seven days later he was playing golf. Specialists checked for signs of brain damage but found none. Further tests revealed that some vision may eventually be restored in the damaged eye. Jason had made a truly miraculous recovery. He returned to college, later married, and in December 1994 his wife gave birth to a son.

Bobby Mescalaro has a young daughter. She was born almost a

year to the day doctors planned to advise disconnecting Bobby
from life-support machinery at a New York hospital. He lay in a
coma for eighteen days after falling sixty feet and suffering the
most appalling injuries imaginable.

Bobby was nineteen at the time, a promising soccer player and
artist. He was repairing iron-work on the balcony of a friend's
apartment when he lost his balance and slipped off the edge. His
fall ended when he smashed head-first into concrete steps in the
alley below.

Both eye sockets and all facial bones were crushed. The skull
bone protruded into the brain in two places. His neck and back
were broken, lung punctured, and heart shifted by the impact. His
right hip and pelvis were smashed. Paramedics were certain they
were looking at a corpse until someone found a faint pulse. During
emergency hospital surgery the neurologist was shocked by the
extent of the damage. Bobby lapsed into a coma. He was totally
paralysed with no realistic chance of recovery.

Parents Eva and Joe Mescalaro were devastated. Doctors had to
sedate Eva, who became distraught at seeing her son's condition.
They were told there was no hope; Bobby could die at any
moment. A priest administered the last rites and Eva and Joe
Mescalaro wrestled with the agonizing decision of whether or not
they should shut down the life-support machine. They chose to
wait. But seventeen days into Bobby's coma Joe Mescalaro called
for the surgeon. 'If my son is the same tomorrow,' he said, 'switch
off the machine.'

Seven hours later a miracle happened.

After some deliberation Eva allowed Bobby's eight-year-old
sister to visit him. She had been reluctant to let Elisabeth see her
brother for fear that it might traumatise her. But Elisabeth wanted
to be with Bobby and Eva agreed. Joe and Eva were standing by
the bed as Elisabeth reached out and stroked her brother's hand. 'I
have been praying for him,' she whispered.

'I know,' said Eva. 'We have all been praying, and Bobby is going to heaven where Jesus will make him better.'

Elisabeth started crying. Her tears fell on to Bobby's hand. 'No, mother,' she said. 'God wants Bobby to come home with us. He doesn't want him in heaven yet.' She squeezed Bobby's fingers. 'Jesus, make him better now!' she shouted.

Eva moved to quieten Elisabeth, but before she had taken one stride across the room Bobby's eyes opened. Eva screamed and collapsed. Joe just froze as Bobby lay looking at Elisabeth. 'Are you better now?' she asked.

Bobby nodded and gently squeezed his sister's hand. Joe Mescalaro began to weep. Within two weeks Bobby was out of intensive care; in another ten days he was back at his parents' home in New Jersey. Medics could offer no rational explanation for the remarkable recovery. They checked and double checked, tested and re-tested but found no lingering signs of brain damage, or any other major long-term damage. Everything broken had been repaired.

Bobby remembers waking from the coma and feeling something like electricity running through his body. 'I did not know where I was,' he recalls. 'I just felt this warm, tingling sensation all over me. It felt as though it was coming from Elisabeth – she was radiant – but the person standing behind her was glowing, really bright, like they were reflecting the sun.'

'And yet there was no one else in the room with us,' Joe Mescalaro insists. 'Just me, your mother and Elisabeth.'

When Bobby thinks of his remarkable recovery today a shiver runs down his spine. 'God sent me an angel,' he says. But when he looks at Elisabeth he adds: 'No, God sent me two angels.'

11

Mediterranean War Theatre

WORLD WAR TWO, 1943

Private James was running through a cloud of red dust when he stepped on a land mine. The explosion blew away most of his leg below the knee.

As he lay in the hot sand, his life ebbing away with his blood, sandflies swarmed over his face. His heart pulsed violently, desperately, and through a red-tinged haze he sensed he was on the rim of death. He believed he had only minutes to live and with his last ounce of strength caught hold of the gold cross around his neck and pulled it free. Private James started to pray.

He was still praying when they found him an hour later. Two soldiers in a jeep spotted him lying face up in the minefield. Carefully negotiating a safe route, they retrieved their injured comrade and took off for the nearest field hospital. One of the soldiers sat in the back of the jeep with Private James. 'He's not going to make it,' he said. 'I can feel a pulse but I think it's flattening out.'

The driver of the jeep put his foot down harder on the gas pedal and the vehicle hurtled along the rough sand track. 'Just hang in there, buddy,' he shouted. 'Just hang in there.'

Private James held the cross of gold tightly in the palm of his hand. He smiled weakly at the soldier who cradled his head in his hands as the jeep bounced and skidded through the desert. He opened his eyes wider and whispered: 'My leg feels warm; it's tingling.'

The soldier glanced at the canvas sheet over the wounded man's legs. He swallowed hard. 'I know. You've been wounded pretty bad,' he said, 'but it'll be okay. The doc will fix you up, you'll see.' But secretly he thought: *If he makes it, he'll be a cripple.*

But something was happening to Private James. Under that blood-stained canvas sheet a miracle was taking place. New body parts were forming. The smashed, mangled flesh and bone had started to repair, mysteriously knitting together to create a new leg and foot. The soldier in the back of the jeep could not see it, but he felt the pulse in Private James' neck strengthen. 'His heart's racing now,' he yelled to the driver. 'I think he's going into shock.'

The jeep raced into the hospital lot and came skidding to a halt. The two soldiers placed Private James on a stretcher and carried him to the operating room. 'He's dying, he needs help now,' the driver told the duty surgeon. 'He's lost a leg, stepped on a mine.' The other soldier said, 'There's nothing left. It's real bad.'

They laid Private James on an operating table. The surgeon checked his pulse and then pulled the canvas sheet back to reveal his legs. 'Is this some kind of joke?' he barked. 'I thought you said he'd lost a leg. This is nothing more than a gashed foot.' The soldiers stepped forward, their mouths agape. The leg and foot had been completely restored. Apart from a wound along the side of the foot there was no sign of any damage from the blast.

Within twelve hours Private James was back on duty. The two soldiers drove him back to where he was stationed. On the way Private James told them about the warm feeling in his leg and the cross of gold that radiated heat as he had held it tightly in his hand. He pulled up the hem on his trousers to examine the new flesh and kicked off his boot to reveal the faintest of scars on his foot. The soldiers could only marvel at a miracle.

12

Under the Cover of the Light

GERMANY, SEPTEMBER 1944

It had been six months since Corrie ten Boom and her sister Betsie had been arrested by the Gestapo. Six months of horrendous suffering at the hands of Hitler's forces. But now they wondered if the nightmare was only just beginning, and the worst was still to come.

From the crest of a hill they gazed fearfully at a vile prison, set in a vast, man-made valley with towering concrete walls all around. At intervals, guards peered down from their observation posts like vultures waiting to pick over the dead. Ahead were the dark menacing shapes of the killing rooms, a grim scar on a green landscape; the smokestack spewing vapour from the furnaces; the skull-and-crossbones staring from the walls beneath electrified wiring.

The giant iron gates swung open to admit the prisoners, then snapped shut again like the jaws of death. Corrie and Betsie were in Ravensbruck, the notorious women's concentration camp. Only God could save them now.

The two women had been convicted of stealing food-ration cards. But they had been helping the Dutch resistance movement in Haarlem, hiding Jewish refugees in a secret room within their home until they could be smuggled out of the country. Hundreds of Jews had been helped, many staying only briefly, others being hidden for months, until on 28 February 1944, Corrie, Betsie and their father were betrayed and arrested.

The Gestapo searched the house, but the secret room had been so cleverly designed that the soldiers found no evidence of hiding and smuggling. When the family refused to reveal the hiding place, for it was still occupied, they were arrested anyway. Stealing food-ration cards carried a minimum six-month prison sentence. It may as well have been a death sentence. Few survived Gestapo punishment.

Casper ten Boom, their eighty-four-year-old father, lived for only ten days after being sentenced – a merciful release, as fifty-nine-year-old Corrie, and Betsie, seven years older, were to discover. In the federal penitentiary of Scheveningen, the concentration camp of Vught, and Ravensbruck, sadism, murder and other monstrous evils were rife.

And yet, through her faith in God and the steadfastness of a spirit that would not be broken, Corrie ten Boom survived, bringing hope and compassion to many suffering prisoners. There in living hell she found strength from heaven; supernatural help that saved her life and the lives and sanity of many others.

Betsie had been born with pernicious anaemia, a debilitating disease of the blood. As a child she frequently had been threatened with pneumonia, and now, approaching old age and frail, she lay on the hard cinder ground outside the buildings, afraid, shivering.

A clap of thunder and a deluge of rain woke her and Corrie, along with the thousand other women prisoners who had bedded down on threadbare blankets and were now sinking into puddles. By daylight they were lying in a swamp, hands, faces and clothes black from the cinder mud.

For two days they were made to stand rigidly to attention on this soggy parade ground, and at night to lie where they had stood, wondering what awaited them within the buildings.

Their only comfort came from their bare provisions: a warm blue sweater, small bottle of vitamin oil, and a precious Bible.

When Betsie began coughing Corrie took the sweater from her pillowcase, wrapped it around her sister and gave her a few drops of the vitamin oil. But by morning Betsie had agonizing intestinal cramps. She was very ill and Corrie breathed a sigh of relief when the order came to report to the Ravensbruck processing centre for new arrivals. It was a harrowing prospect, but at least Betsie had been spared a third night lying out in the chilling damp air on the sodden cinders.

The relief was short-lived. As the two sisters made their way along a corridor into a large reception room they realised they were to be stripped and searched. As each woman reached a desk where officers sat she had to lay her blanket, pillowcase and other belongings on to a growing pile. A few desks further along she had to strip naked, throwing every scrap of clothing on to a second pile, and walk past the scrutiny of a dozen SS men into the shower room. Coming out of the shower room she wore only a thin prison dress and a pair of shoes.

Corrie was horrified. Betsie needed the sweater and the vitamin oil. Both needed the Bible. But how could she ever take it past so many guards? Surely it was impossible? *Dear God*, she prayed, *you have given us this precious Book. You have kept it hidden through many checkpoints and inspections . . .*

They were almost at the first desk when Corrie reached into her pillowcase and drew out the bottle of vitamin oil, closing her fist tightly around it. She started praying, silently, but stopped abruptly when she felt Betsie stagger against her. Her sister's face was white, her lips pressed tight together. Corrie begged one of the guards to allow them to go to the toilets, and without so much as a glance he jerked his head in the direction of the shower room.

An SS man stood guarding the door. 'Please, where are the toilets?' Corrie asked.

He did not look at the two women either. 'Use the drainholes,' he snapped, and as Corrie and Betsie stepped inside he slammed the door. They stood alone in the room. A few minutes later they would return to this place, stripped naked. They looked around and saw a pile of prison dresses inside the door, and stacked in the far corner were old wooden benches, slimy with mildew and crawling with cockroaches.

Corrie knew what to do and acted quickly. 'Take the sweater off!' Betsie handed it to her and Corrie wrapped it around the Bible and bottle of vitamin oil, then hid the bundle behind the benches. Minutes later they returned to this room and stood beneath the cold showers, feeling the icy water soften their lice-eaten skin.

Corrie found a loose long-sleeved dress for Betsie that would eventually cover the blue sweater, then dressed herself before reaching behind the benches to the small bundle, pushing it inside the neck. It made an obvious bulge but she flattened it out, shoving it down and tugging the sweater around her waist. It was still visible beneath the thin cotton dress, but Corrie had the feeling that it did not matter. She was convinced God would blind the watching eyes.

As they walked back out through the shower room door, the SS men ran their hands over every prisoner, front, back and sides. Corrie knew she was taking a huge risk. Bibles were forbidden property. To be found with one meant a doubling of the prison sentence as well as a cutback on rations, which already were close to starvation level.

The woman ahead of Corrie was searched three times. She had hidden a woollen vest under her dress and it was found and confiscated. Behind her, Betsie was searched, but no hand touched Corrie. At the exit door to the building a line of women guards examined each prisoner again. Corrie slowed down as she reached them but the officer in charge shoved her violently.

'Move along! You are holding up the line.' Again, she wasn't searched, and the two sisters arrived at Barracks 8 with their precious belongings ... and a wonderful reminder of God's power.

Weeks passed and incredibly the bottle of vital vitamin oil continued to produce drops. It did not seem possible. The bottle was so small and yet more than a dozen women were taking the precious oil. Vitamin deficiency was one of the worst hazards to prisoners. Instinct told Corrie to hoard it – Betsie was growing weaker – but others were ill, too ill to ignore, and even though Corrie tried to save the oil for the very weakest, these soon numbered more than two dozen. And still, every time she tilted the bottle, a drop emerged. Corrie examined the wet tip of the glass stopper in disbelief. She held the bottle up to the light to see how much oil was left, but the dark brown glass was too thick to see through.

'Maybe only a molecule or two really gets through the pinhole and then in the air it expands,' she told Betsie, trying desperately to explain how the drops continued to fall daily on to the rations of bread.

'Don't try to explain it,' Betsie said. 'Just accept it as a surprise from our loving Father.'

One day another woman prisoner pushed her way to Corrie and Betsie in the food line. 'Look what I have got for you,' she said.

They peered into the small cloth sack she carried. There was a pile of vitamins, stolen from the prison staff room. Back at the bunk Corrie took the bottle of vitamin oil from its hiding place. 'We will finish the drops first,' she said. But no matter how long she held it upside down, or how hard she shook it, not another drop appeared.

Betsie died in prison from starvation and illness. A short time later Corrie was released. Her suffering had ended, but it was not until 1959 that she discovered how God had intervened in order to secure her freedom.

She was revisiting Ravensbruck as part of a pilgrimage, remembering and honouring the ninety-six thousand women who died there, when she learned that her own release had been the result of a clerical error. A week after she had been freed, all the women prisoners of her age had been taken to the gas chambers.

13

Out of the Blue

GALVESTON, GULF OF MEXICO, 1987

Every Sunday for more than twenty-five years Jack Cooley had fished the Gulf waters off the coast of his home town of Galveston. He loved the ocean; he lived for it. Even watching the boats at their moorings gave him pleasure. He liked the way the sun glistened on the masts of the shrimping fleet; liked the gentle creak and groan of the vessels on the morning tide, the sound of water lapping the sea wall.

Jack's father had moved the family to the coast from Navasota, north of Houston, back in 1960. He was a painter and writer and wanted to work beside the sea, and ever since his father first set up a canvas on the south shore Jack had hunted marlin and shark. It was his supreme pleasure.

But today he found no comfort in it.

He had planned to join four friends in the *Mary Rouge* for a day's fishing down past the Matagorda Peninsula where the Texas shore forms the world's longest chain of barrier islands as it slips toward Mexico. But as he sat on the jetty waiting for his buddies, he didn't want to go. He couldn't explain why, but he knew something was wrong. From somewhere deep down in his being a distress signal was being beamed to his senses, and no matter how he tried he could not make the bad feeling go away. He couldn't understand it. He loved to fish, loved the water. But today he was afraid of the sea. For the first time in his life the deep, dark well of her soul put a chill in his heart.

The uneasy feeling had been with him for 24 hours now. Beth Cooley had it too. 'I don't think you should go,' she'd told her husband the previous evening. 'I know it may sound crazy but I can't help thinking that something terrible will happen if you go fishing tomorrow. I've even prayed about it, it's been bothering me that much. I don't know where these awful feelings are coming from, but I'd be happier if you stayed home.'

Jack had told her to calm down. 'How many fishing trips have I made in my life, Beth? Hundreds, thousands maybe, and I'm right here talking to you now.' He laughed shortly. 'Maybe your hormones are acting up, or you're getting paranoid in your old age. Just don't worry about it. I'll be fine.'

Beth, a devout Catholic, wanted to believe him, wanted to convince herself that she was going to feel foolish when Jack returned safely, but she could not. 'Deep down I knew that God was telling me it wasn't safe for Jack to go,' she recalls, 'but I couldn't stop him. I just had to pray and hope God would speak to his heart.'

He did. Come morning, Jack felt uneasy about the trip, then downright scared. By the time he put one foot in the boat he was sweating and shaking, as though he had a fever, and the distress signal deep down inside kept telling him to 'Go home, Jack, go home.' The skipper of the launch thought he looked a sick man when he helped Jack back on to the jetty. 'You must be coming down with something,' he said.

'Maybe I am,' Jack said, wiping beads of perspiration from his forehead. 'But listen, guys. I know this is going to sound pretty strange, but I've got a bad feeling about today. I think maybe you shouldn't go out there. I don't know why, but something's not right and I feel real spooked about it.'

His fishing buddies frowned, then laughed. The skipper said:

'You *are* coming down with something, Jack. Listen, go back home, get to bed, and we'll see you tomorrow.'

But Jack never saw his friends again. Pete Henk, a neighbour, came banging on the door early Monday night. 'Have you heard about the *Mary Rouge*? She hasn't come back in,' he said. 'She's lost at sea; must have gone down. All the wives started getting worried when the boys didn't show up before dusk last night and now they think they're dead.'

Jack felt sick. He looked at Henk. 'I told them not to go. I knew something like this would happen.'

Henk saw tears well up in Jack's eyes. The colour drained from his face. 'What are you talking about, Jack? What are you saying?'

Jack stared at the man on his doorstep. 'I'm saying I had some kind of premonition.'

They found wreckage of the boat four days later, washed up in three places along the Texas shore. There were no survivors, no bodies recovered, and no clues about what happened.

'I was devastated,' Jack recalls. 'I will probably never really get over it. They were my friends and for a long time I couldn't help thinking that maybe I should have done more to stop them going out that day. But at the time I didn't really believe the truth of my conviction. I felt something was wrong, but I guess they thought I was a little crazy.'

'Before it happened I had lost my faith in God: I didn't want to know anything about religion, even though I could see that my wife's relationship with God was real. In the past I had heard her pray for sick friends and watched them miraculously recover. The tragedy made me realise that it's only through God's grace that we live and breathe.'

14

Under a Stormy Sky

SOUTH AFRICA, 1994

They call it the Lanseria Airport miracle, the inexplicable event that many believe prevented the bloodiest of civil wars. It happened in April 1994, just days before South Africa's momentous first ever democratic election, when the odds were stacked against anyone brokering peace in a country which seemed destined to end centuries of racial conflict with a major bloodbath.

It has been estimated that more than a million people would have died if the elections had gone ahead without the participation of the Inkatha Freedom Party. International mediators Dr Henry Kissinger and Lord Carrington had already decided that no breakthrough could be made between the IFP and the African National Congress. The peace process was left teetering on the brink of disaster. And then something happened on a plane high above South Africa. The rest, they say, is history.

It was vital that veteran Kenyan diplomat Washington Okumu met with Chief Mangosuthu Buthelezi, leader of the IFP. They had already spoken briefly after Kissinger and Carrington had aborted the international mediation plan, but now Okumu had devised a plan to make it possible for the IFP to take part in the elections and he had to see Buthelezi, urgently. Okumu's colleague Dr Willem Olivier, advisor to the KwaZulu government, tried to contact Buthelezi in his hotel room to try to arrange the meeting but the Chief had already left town to catch a flight.

Olivier phoned several airports and located Buthelezi's plane at Lanseria. It was on the tarmac and ready to take off. Olivier persuaded the control tower to radio the pilot and ask him to request that the Chief return to the terminal building and wait for Okuma's arrival. Buthelezi agreed and the plane returned.

'I decided to wait for him a little while,' Buthelezi recalls, 'but he didn't arrive. Two of my colleagues with me were going to the Zulu King's palace because there was a meeting scheduled that day between Archbishop Desmond Tutu and a delegation of clergymen who were going to see the King. It worried me that we should not be late for the meeting, so finally I said we should leave.'

Okumu was already on his way by taxi to Lanseria airport. The driver was racing through red lights. 'We must get there,' he told Okumu. 'If the police catch me, I'll tell them what you are doing, and they will give us a full police escort.' But the Chief's plane had already taken off, and Okumu's high-speed ride looked destined to end in disaster.

'We were airborne,' Buthelezi says, 'then the pilot said there was something wrong with the plane. The compass was playing up. And this was a brand new plane. So we had to return to Lanseria. Okumu by now was in the manager's office, having just arrived. I said to him, "You know, my brother, God has brought me back, like Jonah, because now there is something wrong with the plane, and it is obvious he wants us to meet."'

Okumu then told Buthelezi of his plan to make changes concerning the King and the Kingdom to enable the IFP to participate in the elections. The two men talked at length. The conversation was momentous. 'In many ways it was a turning point,' said Okumu later.

Noel Potter, Managing Director of Osprey Aerospace in Johan-

nesburg, whose pilots were on contract to the KwaZulu government, believes the fault on the compass was 'an act of God'. 'It
was so inconceivable,' he says, 'that our pilots, men of huge
experience and capability, could have made an error so basic
relating to the routine alignment on the ground of the plane's two
compass systems. This is required to be performed while the
aircraft is completely stationary. Conceivably in haste, they did
this while the plane was being towed or not quite stationary.
Although very unlikely, this could have resulted in the problem
of the compasses acting up.

'There was a unique sequence of events, each in itself unlikely,
which could have occurred something like this: First, shortly after
take-off, a substantially incorrect compass reading was experienced,
initially thought to be a technical problem with the compass
system. Due to back-up systems, this is not a real problem on its
own.

'Second, however, this problem initiated a sequence of compass
and autopilot "snags" while airborne which, while not in any way
dangerous or life-threatening, required the pilots to land the
aircraft as a matter of precaution.

'Third, there was the unique timing of events so that a turnback
to Lanseria, rather than a diversion to another airfield, was the
logical action for the aircrew to take. The plane had been airborne
for only eight minutes. Had the problem manifested itself a few
minutes later, the plane would have been rerouted to land at
another airport and not at Lanseria where Professor Okumu was
waiting.'

When Osprey performed the postflight check of the new
compass systems for the suspected technical problems, none was
found. Potter says: 'The only conceivable explanation for the
problem is that the experienced and highly meticulous crew,
through a very unlikely omission in the preflight compass alignment procedure, set in motion the extraordinary chain of events

which ultimately resulted in Chief Buthelezi's timely return to Lanseria. But it doesn't really add up. The pilot was mystified, too, and said that as far as he was concerned it was an "act of God", especially when we later discovered what flowed from the subsequent conversation between Professor Okumu and Chief Buthelezi.'

Many believe Buthelezi was right when, in his press statement on the occasion of the signing of the Peace (Election) Agreement, he said: 'I told Professor Okumu that my forced return was a Godsend.'

15

Rupe and the Preacher

SEATTLE, USA, 1960

Rupe was a big, friendly man who was dying and had lost his faith in God. Rupe was also the son of a minister, but when the preacher asked him, 'Do you believe in Jesus?' he said, 'No, sir, I don't. I can find no record of his ever having existed.'

It was an honest answer because Rupe was an honest man, the kind of guy it is hard not to like. He had a kind, generous heart, even though it was displaced so far that it was on the wrong side of his chest. It was not the only thing wrong with him.

Rupe had been sent to hospital with severe pain which the doctor diagnosed as kidney stones. What the doctor didn't know was that Rupe also had a seriously infected appendix, and while he was being treated for the kidney problem the appendix ruptured. The infection had virtually destroyed his diaphragm, the muscular wall that separates the abdominal cavity from the chest cavity and serves as the main breathing muscle. One lung was collapsed. Rupe was in a bad way.

'The doctors tell me I'll be on a respirator soon,' he told the preacher. 'They say I probably won't live too long. My diaphragm is like a limp rag; it's not only paralysed, it's full of holes. They can't believe that I am able to breathe at all. It seems I've learned to use my rib muscles for breathing. Right now my voice is weakened by this, and it's too high in pitch, which is a serious handicap in my profession.'

The preacher was not put off. 'Will you come to our prayer meeting tonight?' he asked.

Rupe thought about it. The church print shop had agreed to help produce a brochure promoting a reading institute Rupe was trying to establish. *I've got to say yes; they're saving me about two hundred dollars.* It was the least Rupe could do, even though he didn't care much for prayer.

That night he found himself sitting there at the meeting, listening and watching. One person after another stood up and testified to God's healing power. The preacher noted that there were more healing testimonies than usual. Rupe just sat there, unbelieving.

'I burned my finger badly last night while I was cooking the dinner,' one woman said, 'but my husband prayed for it, and look, it isn't even red.'

A man reported: 'I smashed my thumb working in my shop. It was all black and blue, but I prayed for it myself, and when I got up this morning there wasn't a sign of a bruise. Look. My doctor says it's impossible. Isn't that great?'

'I had to leave my glasses off,' a woman said, 'because as God began to heal my eyes, soon I couldn't see with my glasses *on!*'

Rupe was still unconvinced. But he was no longer impassive; something deep inside, soul deep, was beginning to stir. He felt the unmistakable tingling sensation of tears forming, and he was having to clench his teeth and swallow to stop himself crying.

A young girl stood up. Rupe looked at her, part of him not wanting to hear any more. She started telling the story of how she had slipped on rocks and cracked her ankle while hiking up a creek bed during a church youth camp one summer. The foot swelled up, she recalled, turning black and blue.

'They took me to the doctor and he X-rayed my ankle,' she said. 'It was broken and he told me to stay on crutches and put no weight on the ankle at all. As soon as the swelling had gone down, the doctor said he would put a cast on it. It didn't sound like much fun to be spending the week at camp on crutches, so I said to two of my friends: "At home the folks would pray for this ankle to be healed."

'So we all went into the chapel, and they laid their hands on my foot, and we asked God to heal it. It stopped hurting right away. I didn't need the crutches any more, so I put them down and went out and joined a baseball game. By that night all the swelling had gone, and by next morning the black and blue was all gone too! The camp nurse and the clergy were pretty unhappy with me because I wouldn't use my crutches. In fact, they wrote a letter to my mother saying that they couldn't be responsible, and the insurance wouldn't cover my injury because I was refusing to co-operate in the treatment.'

The girl sat down and the preacher saw Rupe get up and leave. He slipped out and caught up with him just as he got into his car. The preacher climbed into the seat beside Rupe and saw that he was close to tears.

'I don't believe the things those people were saying in there are possible,' Rupe said. 'I don't believe in that sort of thing.'

He turned to face the preacher. 'So why did I weep while they were saying them?' Rupe paused, taking a deep breath, then cried: 'Can you heal my diaphragm?'

'No, I can't,' the preacher answered, 'but God can.' He put his hand on Rupe's shoulder and prayed. 'Dear God, we sure could use a miracle right about now.' But nothing visible happened and as Rupe drove away the preacher thought: 'Well, that will probably confirm him in his unbelief. Too bad.'

A week passed, and the preacher had almost forgotten about Rupe until the big, friendly man walked into the prayer meeting once again. He was smiling; beaming, in fact.

Perhaps he's come to laugh at us, the preacher thought, feeling slightly uncomfortable. But he was wrong, very wrong. As soon as the time came to share, Rupe was on his feet. He told about the prayer the preacher had said in the car the week before, and then he went on: 'Nothing seemed to happen that night, but yesterday my son and I were crossing the Sound on the ferry when suddenly a terrific pain hit me in the diaphragm. I felt it tighten up, and I've been breathing normally ever since.'

Rupe went back to the doctor, who was curious to find out how his patient was breathing normally without a diaphragm. He asked for an X-ray moving picture to be made of Rupe's abdomen. The result shocked him. 'Your diaphragm is still full of holes; it's still a mess,' he said. 'But it's working again!'

Rupe found the faith he had lost. He still could not accept the existence of God intellectually, but he clearly saw God's power, and he could not deny it. Then he began to have other prayers answered, and it was not long before Rupe started to change his mind. He couldn't fight the feeling any longer; every fibre of his being sensed God was real. He just knew it.

Two years later, Rupe was praying at home with two friends. Suddenly one of them said: 'My hands are on fire. They are hurting me.'

'Put them on me,' Rupe answered, moving closer, and his friend placed his hands on the big man's chest.

'Suddenly I felt as though all my insides had fallen out,' Rupe recalls. 'I sprang to my feet and literally had to grab my trousers to keep them from falling off; they were suddenly too loose. I had to struggle to get my coat unbuttoned; it was now too tight. The whole outward configuration of my body was changing as my internal organs were renewed and went back into their proper positions. My heart was thumping like a hammer and I felt it move three or four inches, back into its proper place under my breastbone. Not only was my diaphragm restored, but my physical body was changed so much that I had to get all new suits.'

16

Light in the Black

ENGLAND, TOWARD THE END OF
THE LAST CENTURY

Rain lashed the windows of the steam train as the beam of its powerful lamp bored into the deep winter night. Up ahead, thick fog smothered the track, and on exposed stretches a violent wind gusted, rocking the carriages.

The driver of the train could not have known it, but they were on a collision course with disaster – and Queen Victoria was one of his passengers.

Suddenly the driver saw something – someone – caught in the beam of the headlight: a strange figure in a black cloak stood in the middle of the tracks waving his arms. The driver grabbed for the brake and brought the train to a grinding halt.

He climbed down from the engine, feeling the chill of the night touch his face as he looked down the tracks to see what had stopped them. But there was no trace of the strange figure. It had disappeared.

The driver sensed something was wrong. He had definitely seen someone or something standing there. On a hunch he walked a short distance further up the tracks. Suddenly he stopped and stared into the fog in horror.

The bridge which his train had been about to cross had been washed out and had collapsed into the roaring waters of the swollen river. If the driver had not stopped for the ghostly figure, the train would have plummeted into the torrent.

While the bridge and the tracks were being repaired, the crew of the train made a more intensive search for the figure in the black cloak. But it wasn't until the train arrived in London that the mystery was solved.

At the base of the engine's headlamp the driver discovered an enormous dead moth. He studied it for a moment, then on impulse wet its wings and pasted it to the glass of the lamp.

Climbing back into his cab, he switched on the lamp and saw the cloaked figure in its beam. He shook his head in disbelief. The moth, he reasoned, had flown into the beam shortly before the train would have plunged into the river. In the fog, the nocturnal insect had appeared to be a phantom figure, waving its arms.

When Queen Victoria was told of the strange incident she said: 'I am sure it was no accident. It was God's way of protecting us.'

The driver knew something extraordinary had taken place during the storm that night, something that had probably saved his life and the life of his Queen. *Maybe one of God's angels placed the moth on the headlight,* he mused. *Maybe I have just witnessed a miracle.*

17

Father Heart

Jonathan White sat at the kitchen table reading the newspaper. It was midnight and he was staring red-eyed at the jobs page. He'd been over it twice already but thought maybe there was something he'd missed. No such luck. He closed the paper and tossed it across the table. 'I'm sick of this crap,' he murmured. He wanted to shout – wanted to throw more than the newspaper – but Jenny and the kids were sleeping and he didn't want to wake them.

Slumping forward, he cradled his head in his hands and let out a tired, frustrated sigh, followed by a deep yawn that made his neck cramp and eyes water. Before he went to bed he picked up the paper and threw it in the bin.

Jonathan had been out of work for twelve months. In his last job he'd worked as an electrician for a shipping firm at the local docks, but he could turn his hand to joinery, plumbing, bricklaying – any of the manual trades. His wife said he was brilliant at all of them. To encourage him she would say, 'Something will come up, you'll see,' but it never did, and just lately he'd begun to wonder if he would ever work again. Had he become nothing more than a government statistic? A member of the chronically unemployed?

The thought frightened him. 'The longer this goes on, the harder it's going to get,' he frequently told Jenny. 'You don't understand, you don't know what it's like. It's a nightmare, a flamin' nightmare. There's never anything in the job centre, nothing in the paper. I mean, I'm a qualified electrician, for Pete's sake. There must be *some* work out there. If I stop believing that, I think I'll crack up.'

The Whites lived in an ex-council house next to a park on the outskirts of the city. It was a nice part of town. The street was pretty, tree-lined and always full of noisy kids tearing around on bikes, skipping, playing football. Jonathan had done the house up really well after he and Jenny had bought it from the council. Double-glazing, new front door and a red-brick drive made it stand out from the rest.

Jenny was delighted with the improvements. For years she had struggled to raise her family on a shoestring, until Jonathan was employed by the shipping firm and his wages doubled. Then she wanted a better standard of living, especially for the kids.

Everything was working out fine until the shipping firm went belly-up and Jonathan was laid-off. Now they were six months behind with the mortgage, the bank was threatening repossession, and they were struggling to feed and clothe the children. Times were hard, extremely hard, and although Jenny would never admit to it, she couldn't see a way out. The future looked bleak.

The kids didn't understand, but why should they? Billy was only seven years old, Sandra was four and Jonathan junior, eighteen months. It would be Christmas in six weeks and they were beginning to get excited. Jonathan was dreading it. Jenny kept telling him not to worry, but he would say, 'How can I give my family a proper Christmas when I'm skint? We won't even be able to afford a decent tree.'

Both he and Jenny had been priming the kids for weeks. 'There won't be a lot this year; Mummy and Daddy haven't got much money, so there won't be as many presents as last Christmas.' But the message didn't sink in. Billy was often to be seen walking around the house with his favourite shopping catalogue in tow. 'That's the one I want, Dad,' he'd say, pointing to a brilliant-red mountain bike on one of the glossy pages.

'I'm glad they don't know the truth,' Jonathan said as he snuggled up to Jenny in bed one night.

'They're just kids,' said Jenny. 'It doesn't matter to them. My mum and dad never had any money and I had a happy childhood. Don't worry about them, Jon. As long as we're both there for them, and love them, that's all that really matters.'

'But what about the house? What about the money we owe? The bank won't wait for ever. You heard that mortgage bloke the other day – reckons it's best if we sell up and rent somewhere. All the money and work we've put into this place, it's just been for nothing.' Jonathan turned over, moving away from Jenny, and looked at the ceiling.

'I'm glad we never decorated in here . . . and I wish we hadn't done the bathroom.'

Jenny gave a groan. 'If you're going to start all that again, then go downstairs. Go and watch TV or something.' She pulled the quilt over her head. 'Oh, I forgot – the TV's got to go back as well, hasn't it?'

'What's that?' Jonathan couldn't quite make out the muffled words. 'What did you say?' he asked.

'Forget it,' she replied, pulling the quilt tighter. 'I just want to go to sleep.'

Jonathan felt rage rising inside him. He sat bolt upright and violently ripped the quilt from Jenny's face. 'You can't go to sleep,' he growled.

She cowered. 'Why not?'

'Because it doesn't make things better.'

'And this does?' Jenny tried to pull the quilt back over her head but Jonathan snatched it out of her hand and threw it on to the floor.

'You just don't understand,' he said. 'You just think things are going to get better and everyone's gonna live happily ever after. Well, wake the hell up and face the truth. We've had it. No one's gonna wave a magic wand and make it all go away. We're done for, but who gives a damn? Let's just go to sleep and forget it.'

Jenny was sobbing. It was getting worse, much worse. The violent mood swings frightened her, they frightened the kids, but she felt helpless. *I know his pain*, she thought. *I know what he's going through.*

Jonathan grabbed her by the throat. She choked. 'Don't cry!' he growled. 'Stop trying to make me feel guilty.'

Jenny tried to force his hand away; she couldn't breathe. 'Jonathan, please, let go.' She squeezed the words out. 'Please stop it.'

He released his grip. 'Oh, God, Jenny, what am I doing, what's happening? I must be going crazy.' Tears filled his eyes and he started crying; desperate, uncontrollable sobbing. The pain was so intense, and it went so deep, that he felt his heart would explode.

Jenny sat up. Her throat was still burning but she only felt her husband's pain. She put her arms around him and pulled his head down to rest on her breasts. She stroked his hair and kissed him tenderly. *If you can hear me, God, please help*, she prayed silently, *I'm holding a broken man and don't know what to do.*

Jonathan was looking out of the window watching the rain clouds rolling in. He saw Billy standing by the front gate, talking to his friend Joshua. The first drops of rain spattered against the glass. Jonathan opened the window. 'Billy, come on, it's going to throw it down in a minute.'

Billy looked up at the window. 'I've got to go,' he told Joshua.

'What about church?' Joshua asked.

'I'll ask him, but it'll be okay, he won't mind,' said Billy.

The heavens opened and Jonathan banged on the window. 'Come on,' he shouted, 'you'll get soaked.'

'See you,' Billy said and ran up the path. He stopped and turned around. 'Josh, Josh. Do I have to pay to get in?'

'What, church? Course not, it's free.'

'He wants to go to church? Who with?' Jenny stood by the gas cooker, heating baked beans.

'Joshua, across the street. The McCreerys go to that New Life place down past the park on the main road,' said Jonathan.

'Oh, the big white building by the school. Yes, Jean goes there. You remember Jean, used to live in number nine. She's okay.' Jenny stirred the beans. 'She said that when her husband died the people down there really helped her. They're Pentecostals or something. The vicar, or whatever they call him, took assembly at Billy's school a few months ago. Billy's teacher said the kids loved it.'

'So what do you think, then?' Jonathan asked.

'Josh is a nice kid, and I like his mum, Paula, although she keeps herself to herself,' said Jenny. 'Billy might really enjoy it. He says they play table tennis after Sunday school and they get squash and sweets. I'll pop across to see Josh's mum later, just to make sure it's all right.'

Jonathan nodded. 'But make sure it doesn't cost anything. You know what these places are like, they expect you to put money in the collection. And tell Billy if he has to pay for the sweets and stuff he can't have any.'

Billy couldn't believe how many kids were in Sunday school. *More than in my class at school*, he thought.

He'd walked down to the New Life centre with Josh and his mum. It had snowed in the night and by the time they arrived at the church his feet were soaked. There were holes in his shoes and his toes ached with the cold.

Billy sat at the back of the room with his feet pressed against a radiator. Paula had taken his shoes and put them somewhere to dry and Billy was enjoying the heat on his toes.

Paula had gone into the main church hall, where the adult service took place. Billy sat next to Joshua in the Sunday school room and listened to a man talk about Jesus. He read from a Bible and told the story of how Jesus fed thousands of people with only five loaves of bread and two small fish. Billy loved it.

'You see, kids, Jesus had compassion for those people,' said the man. 'They'd been on the side of a mountain with him for three days, watching Jesus heal people – the blind, the dumb, the crippled. Jesus had done all these miracles but he didn't want to send the people away hungry. He was concerned that some of them might collapse on the way home. The disciples didn't think it was possible to feed so many people with so little food, but Jesus made it possible because he is the son of God. And, you know, kids, Jesus is still working miracles in people's lives today, because he loves each and every one of us.'

Afterwards Billy played table-tennis with Joshua, but he couldn't stop thinking about what the man had said. One of the Sunday school teachers had given each of the kids a packet of sweets. Billy didn't eat his; he wanted to save them for Sandra and Jonathan junior. It was ages since they'd had any sweets. Paula fetched Billy's dry shoes and stuffed plastic bags in them to keep his feet dry on the way home.

'Did you have a nice time?' asked Paula.

'Yes, it was great,' said Billy. 'I enjoyed it, especially the story. Can I come again?'

'Of course you can. We'd like that, Josh, wouldn't we?'

Josh nodded and looked at Billy's shoes. 'Can't you afford any new ones?' he asked.

'I don't know,' Billy replied. 'My dad's getting me a mountain bike for Christmas, so I guess I'll have to wait.'

On the way home Billy asked God for a miracle. He didn't say it aloud but prayed silently. *Do a miracle in our house, please, God. We've got no food and no money. My dad's angry all the time and my mum cries alone in the bathroom. I know you know all these things but if your son Jesus can feed all those people with just a bit of bread and some fish then you could easily do a miracle in our house, please.*

It was two days later, on a night when Jonathan and Jenny were fighting, that Billy's prayer was answered. Jonathan stormed out of the back door and tripped over a large, rectangular wicker basket. 'Jesus!' he said sprawling across the back yard. 'Who the hell put that there?'

Jenny heard the commotion and rushed to the back door. She saw the wicker basket and looked at Jonathan, sitting on the floor in the dark. 'You'll catch a chill,' she said, smiling.

'It's not funny,' he snapped. 'I could have broken my neck.'

'That was the idea. I was thinking of the insurance money!' Jenny started laughing.

Jonathan sprang to his feet. 'Go on, laugh, why don't you. It's dead funny, if not hilarious. So you put it there, eh?'

She glared at him. 'No, I didn't. I haven't got a clue where it came from. It wasn't there earlier on.'

The noise had woken the kids. Now Billy and Sara stood on the back step. Billy was holding Jonathan junior. 'What's up, mum?' he said.

'Dad fell over something, that's all,' she answered. 'We'd better get it inside and find out what it is.'

Jonathan walked around the basket, prodding the sides with his foot. He ran his hand across the top, lifting it slightly to feel its weight. 'Grief, it's heavy!'

The lid was fastened down with a metal clasp and wooden peg. Jonathan loosened the peg, pushed it out and flicked the clasp up. He opened the lid a few inches, peered inside, then shut it quickly. 'Get it indoors,' he ordered. 'Come on, hurry up.'

'What's inside?' asked Jenny. 'What is it?'

Jonathan grabbed one of the handles. 'Just help me get it inside and you'll find out.'

The kids watched anxiously as their parents dragged the basket over the step and into the kitchen.

Jonathan slammed the door shut and threw open the lid. 'It's a food hamper!' he shouted. 'A Christmas food hamper!'

Jenny and the kids just stood there, gazing open-mouthed at the basket of food in front of them. It was enormous, and packed with tins, packets, bags and bottles of food and drink. There was an envelope tucked inside the lid. Jenny took it out, opened the envelope, and read the note. 'Happy Christmas and God Bless.' She just stared at it, reading the words over and over again.

'Let me have a look,' Jonathan said, snatching the paper from Jenny. He turned the paper over to see if there was anything on the other side. 'Is that it? Nothing else in the envelope?'

'No, that's it,' said Jenny. 'I can't believe it, there must be hundreds of pounds' worth of stuff in there. Who'd do a thing like this? I mean, why? Just look at it, Jonathan, just look.'

'I am, I am, there must be enough food in here to last us until Easter. I just can't believe it, I just can't take it in.' Jonathan looked at the hamper, then at the kids. He reached into the basket and pulled out a box of chocolates. 'Here you are, kids, share these,' he said, tearing off the wrapper. 'Santa's come early.'

But Billy knew differently. *It's a miracle, God has done a miracle,* he thought. *Thank you for answering my prayer, Jesus. I didn't know if you could but I'm glad you did, because this is great. Thank you, God, thank you.*

Billy went back to church the following Sunday, but he didn't tell Joshua or anyone else about the food hamper. It was between him and God. His mum and dad could not explain where it had come from. For days they talked about it, but in the end simply accepted it. 'It's strange, really weird,' Jonathan said, 'but I'm not complaining. It's made our Christmas. I guess someone up there likes us.'

After Sunday school Joshua gave Billy a guided tour of the church. 'This is where the pastor preaches,' he said, standing behind an impressive brass and glass lectern in the shape of a soaring eagle. 'One day my mum was here in the church, after my dad had left us and we had no money, and the pastor said that God was going to help someone who had no money. The next day we got a cheque from dad. He never sent us money before and once told my mum he didn't care if we starved, but God must have told him to help us.'

Billy listened. He liked Joshua and felt sorry for him, being without a dad. 'It must have been a miracle,' he said.

'Yes, it was,' said Josh, 'but God does them all the time. My mum says God loves to give gifts to everyone who loves him, and sometimes he does things for people who don't believe in him.'

'Why?' asked Billy.

'He just does,' said Joshua. 'I guess he just really cares about people, that's all.'

'I believe you,' Billy said. 'I believe God does miracles, and I've already asked him to give my mum and dad some extra money so they don't have to worry about things when Christmas comes, and I've asked for a job for my dad. I know he'll do it because he's already answered one of my prayers.'

Josh jumped down from the lectern and grabbed Billy's arm. 'Come on,' he said, 'there's cakes and stuff in the other room.' Billy ran after him, whooping.

Jenny let out a shriek. 'Oh, my God! There must be some mistake.' The people queuing behind Jenny in the building society looked at each other, and then at the cashier. 'There is too much money here, you've made a mistake.' Jenny composed herself and handed a slip of paper back to the girl behind the counter.

'I'll check it,' said the girl, and she entered Jenny's account details into the computer. The machine reacted, and a second printed balance slip emerged. The girl handed the paper to Jenny. 'Everything okay?' she asked.

Jenny stared at the print-out in disbelief. She was speechless.

'Mrs White, are you okay? Is there something wrong?'

Jenny moved as close to the counter as she could. The girl leaned forward. 'Look right here,' Jenny said, pointing to the slip of paper. 'It says there's a thousand pounds in my account. It must be wrong because we've only got thirty pounds. Please will you do it again?'

The girl smiled. 'Mrs White, the amount on your statement is correct. It can't be wrong. Perhaps you're mistaken and you have more money than you thought. But if you like I'll check it with the manager. I'll be right back.'

She kept looking at the paper and shaking her head. The girl returned, smiling. 'Yes, that figure is correct. There was a deposit this morning. I take it you weren't expecting it.'

'No,' said Jenny, 'I wasn't. I still can't believe it. Where has it come from, can you tell me?'

'I could try to find out.'

'No, it doesn't matter,' said Jenny, still bemused. 'I'll pop back later . . . to see if it's still there!'

Jenny flew home. She had to tell Jonathan about the money before he left for the job centre. But Jonathan was going nowhere. He was already in a state of shock. Sara and Jonathan junior were playing on the kitchen floor when Jenny burst through the door. 'Where's your dad?' she gasped.

'He's upstairs,' said Sara. 'A nice man gave him a job.'

Jenny was stopped in her tracks. 'What did you say, Sara?' There was a slight tremble in her voice.

'Daddy's got a job, mending electricity. The nice man came to the house, and Daddy started crying,' Sara said. 'I think they were happy tears.'

Jenny heard Jonathan coming down the stairs so she sat down. He had a huge smile on his face. 'You're not going to believe what's happened,' he said.

'Tell me,' said Jenny.

Jonathan sat down next to his wife and held her hand. 'Well, this bloke, John Adams, came to the house just after you went out. I never saw him before in my life, hadn't got a clue who he was. He tells me he owns this building firm near Southport, and was I interested in working for him? I couldn't believe it. I mean, I never saw him before in my life. Then, right out of the blue, he pulls my business card out of his pocket – one of those I had printed before I got the job at the docks. Says he found it in his desk.'

'But how did he know you hadn't got a job already?' Jenny asked.

'Well, this is the really weird bit,' Jonathan said. 'Mr Adams is one of those born again Christian people – you know, like Paula. He says God told him to get in touch with me. Honest, that is what he said. But that's not all, Jen; last night, before he decided to come here, one of the electricians who had worked for him for years quit. He's got another job, and I'm taking over from him! Mr Adams says it was confirmation that God wanted me to work for him. Weird, eh?'

'I'm just gobsmacked,' said Jenny, 'but how do you know he's not a crank. I mean, is he genuine?'

'That's what I said to him; he could have been a nutter, but his firm's in the *Yellow Pages*; they've been in business for years. I checked it; he told me to. And he's given me a contract, says I can take it to a solicitor to get it checked before I sign it. It's real, Jen, 100 per cent. I told him about the food hamper as well; I felt as though I had to. He says God is blessing this house. Can you believe that?'

Jenny started crying. She was clutching their savings book. 'I believe it, Jon. I don't know what's happening or why, but something special is happening to us, and I think it's got something to do with Billy going to church. I know you say you don't believe in God or anything like that, but I believe the food hamper and you getting a job are real miracles – and you had better look at this.'

She passed the savings book to Jonathan. 'Look at the balance,' she said.

Her husband looked at the book in amazement. 'A thousand pounds? It must be a mistake!' He was visibly shaken.

Jenny beamed. 'No, it's not a mistake. The girl at the building society checked it three times. It's another miracle, Jon.'

Jonathan tried to hold back the tears. He didn't know what was happening, but deep inside he felt something breaking. It was like a dam bursting, the flood-gates of his soul opening, and the tears fell. He couldn't stop them. 'Jesus, Jesus, Jesus,' he sobbed. 'Thank you, thank you, Jesus.' The words came from his heart. His mind could not grasp them, and he knew right then that another miracle was taking place. God was mending a broken life.

18

Silent World

People who did not know what had happened to little Lucy Browne used to think she was not like other children. They saw the vacant stare and the painful frown and believed she must be retarded in some way. Some thought the girl was born deaf and dumb because there were times when Lucy did not respond at all. Others accused her of being ignorant and rude.

It was not their fault they didn't understand. How could they possibly know her pain? How could they feel the fear in her dark world? Lucy Browne had locked herself away in the deepest, most secret part of her mind. Fear and pain had stolen her words. She hadn't spoken since her father died and there was no way of knowing if she would speak again.

Henry Browne died in a car crash the day after Lucy's sixth birthday. Lucy stopped talking the day after the funeral. Paula Browne was afraid for her daughter but people told her not to worry. 'It's natural shock. Lucy will be okay in a couple of days,' they said. But Lucy wasn't. Her silence continued for days, weeks, months. Doctors dismissed fears of long-term psychological damage. Child psychologists predicted recovery, and Paula was asked to let time heal her daughter. 'It's Lucy's way of dealing with the loss of her father,' they said. 'It is not permanent; she will start to speak again.'

Paula took Lucy out of school. Other children had started to torment her and Lucy withdrew deeper into her secret place. Paula gave up work to devote all her time to Lucy, who spent most of her time watching television or playing with her toys. Paula showered her daughter with love and affection, talked to her about Henry's death, and how he would have wanted them to be happy in their lives afterwards.

But there was no way in, no way through the barrier of silence, and Paula became despondent. Her daughter would not open up, she would not respond to anyone or anything.

One day in desperate frustration Paula lashed out. It had all become too much, and she smacked Lucy across the face. But the child did not cry, did not utter one sound, and the hurt destroyed another piece of Paula's heart.

Six months passed and despite regular visits to a child psychologist Lucy remained isolated in her silent world. Doctors assured Paula that her daughter was essentially a healthy, growing child. Lucy was eating and sleeping – 'positive signs', they insisted. She was just unwilling to communicate, for the time being.

'Does Lucy talk to herself?' they asked. Paula had already established that she did not. 'I have spied on her many times,' she told them, 'but I have never seen or heard Lucy speak. Even when she plays with her dolls she is silent. I have stood outside her bedroom door for an hour or more sometimes, hoping, praying for a word, just one word, but she never speaks.'

Paula was losing hope. She was afraid Lucy would not speak again, and in her desperation turned to the church. 'I'm not a religious woman,' she told the priest who had buried Henry, 'but I believe in God and believe that he can help Lucy. Nothing else has worked and I'm scared. She seems okay, but I am afraid that she is suffering inside, unable to break free from whatever it is that is preventing her from opening up. She hasn't shed a tear since Henry died.'

The priest listened and agreed to help. 'I believe in miracles,' he told Paula. 'They are not confined to the pages of the Bible, not at all. God is still in the business of healing people, and he sees the seed of faith in your heart, Paula. Your faith shall heal Lucy. Have you a handkerchief?'

The priest's question puzzled Paula. 'A handkerchief? Yes, in my handbag, I think. But why?'

The priest smiled. 'It's not such a strange request. We use handkerchiefs as channels for God's healing power. It's a faith thing.'

The priest reached for a Bible. 'Let me read to you from God's Word, to help you understand, Paula. Don't look worried; I am not about to preach a sermon.' He laughed. 'I'm not one who likes the sound of his own voice.'

He found Acts chapter 19 and read: '"God did extraordinary miracles through Paul" – Paul the apostle, that is – "so that even handkerchiefs and aprons that had touched him were taken to the sick, and their illnesses were cured and evil spirits left them."'

When the priest looked up from the Bible, Paula had tears in her eyes. 'You know,' he added, 'Jesus said: "What things you desire when you pray, believe that you receive them, and you shall have them." Let's ask God to heal Lucy.'

Paula took out a handkerchief and the priest prayed over it. 'Lay it on Lucy's pillow,' he said, 'and I will look forward to hearing Lucy singing in church on Sunday.'

At home Paula tucked the handkerchief into Lucy's pillow hoping, praying for a miracle. That night the little girl slept soundly, but Paula could not settle. Nothing else had helped. Why should this? Twice during the night she crept into Lucy's room to watch her sleeping child. It was well into the early hours when Paula finally fell into a fitful sleep, the words of the priest gently echoing in her troubled mind: 'God is still in the business of healing people.'

She awoke to find Lucy standing by the side of the bed. Lucy had been crying! There were tear stains on her cheeks. Paula suddenly remembered the handkerchief. 'Lucy, are you okay? What's the matter, sweetheart?'

Lucy did not answer. She just stood there and started to cry again. Paula curled her arms around her and held her tight. Lucy started weeping, sobbing uncontrollably. Paula lifted Lucy's head and placed her fingers on the child's lips. 'Tell me you love me, Lucy,' she said.

'I do, I do love you, Mummy,' Lucy sobbed.

With those words the dam broke in Paula's heart.

Soon they were sobbing together.

19

Kelly's Hero

NORTHERN ENGLAND, 1985

Elisabeth Kelly believes an angel saved the life of her daughter during the summer of 1985. Those who witnessed the accident say there is no way anyone could have survived.

It was late one Friday afternoon when Elisabeth decided to visit her friend Nancy. On the way she planned to buy milk at the corner shop where her mother worked. Nancy always seemed to be out of milk when Elisabeth visited. *No black tea or coffee today*, she thought. *This time I'm going prepared.*

Elisabeth's daughter, Maria, was excited. She would be five the following day and Nancy was sure to have a birthday present waiting for her. 'Let's take the short cut, Mummy,' she said. But Elisabeth was already heading toward the shop.

It was busy at the crossroads and Elisabeth couldn't find a parking space. 'We're going to be late,' she said, glancing at the clock on the dashboard. 'Nancy leaves for aerobics at five and it's four already. Maybe I should have phoned first.'

'I told you we should have gone the other way, Mummy,' said Maria.

There was no way Elisabeth was going to drive any further to look for a parking space, so she swung the car hard over to the right and pulled up, half on the kerb, on the opposite side of a blind corner.

'Wait in the car, Maria. I won't be a minute,' she said, and ran across the road and into the shop.

Victoria Kelly was arranging jars of jam when her daughter burst into the shop. 'Hi, Mum,' she said, 'just popped in for some milk. We're on our way to Nancy's.'

'Where's Maria?' Victoria asked anxiously. 'You haven't left her in the car, have you? I keep telling you it's not safe.'

Elisabeth rolled her eyes. 'She's fine, Mum. I'll only be a minute. Where's the milk?'

'There's a couple of bottles left, right at the back of the fridge,' Victoria said, wiping her hands on her apron and heading for the door. 'I'm going out to Maria.'

Elisabeth had just opened the fridge door when she heard her mother scream out Maria's name. She raced out of the shop to see Victoria standing on the pavement, holding her granddaughter. That same instant the air shook, with a resounding crash.

Down the street a truck had smashed into the front of Elisabeth's car, sending it spinning into a wall and crushing it against the stonework.

Elisabeth felt nauseous and fainted.

When she came to she was sitting in a chair in the back room of the corner shop. Maria was perched on a radiator shelf, sucking a red lollipop. Victoria stood in the doorway talking to a policeman. Elisabeth let out a faint groan and they all turned to look.

'Mrs Kelly,' said the police officer, 'are you feeling okay?'

Elisabeth nodded and smiled at Maria.

'Our car's been smashed, Mummy,' said the little girl. 'How are we going to get to Nancy's?'

'Never mind that now, honey,' Victoria said, lifting Maria off the shelf. 'Go and give your mum a big hug.'

Elisabeth sat up and embraced her daughter, tears spilling down her cheeks. 'How did you get out of the car?' she asked. 'I thought I told you not to ... Well, thank God you weren't in the car. Thank God you're okay.'

Maria took the lollipop from her mouth. 'Don't cry, Mummy,' she said. 'A nice giant man got me out and carried me to the shop before the lorry came and ran into our car. He was really tall.' She stretched her arm up toward the ceiling. 'He was taller than this, taller than the police officer, much taller, and he had long golden hair and silver clothes.'

Elisabeth felt a knot tighten in her chest. She glanced at the officer. 'I locked the doors,' she said. 'I know it was stupid, but I locked her in and was gone less than a minute. Who was he?'

The policeman coughed. 'We're not sure. I've asked if anyone saw this man take your daughter from the car, but apart from this lady here, no one did.'

Elisabeth looked at her mother. 'You saw him? Mum, what did you see? What happened?'

Victoria looked slightly bemused. 'I'm not sure, dear. I just saw this man carrying Maria across the road. He was tall, and he did have long golden hair. He walked right up to me and put Maria down on the pavement.'

Elisabeth blinked. 'What did he say? What did he do?'

'He didn't say or do anything. I bent down to get hold of Maria, and when I looked up he wasn't there. He'd disappeared. Vanished into thin air.'

'Are you sure?' asked the police officer, opening his notebook. 'Are you sure he didn't just cross the road or walk back up the street? Maybe you lost sight of him.'

Victoria laughed. 'He was seven feet tall, taller perhaps, and he was wearing bright shiny clothes, like a long robe.' She paused. 'I may be getting old, but I'm not blind or stupid. I'm telling you he simply vanished.'

Elisabeth wiped her eyes. 'Whoever he was, he saved Maria's life – but how could he have known she was in danger? I mean, you just don't walk up to someone's car and take a child out without a good reason. Anyway, the doors were locked.' She shook her head. 'I just can't believe it.'

Maria had finished her lollipop and was chewing the cardboard stick. 'I can believe it,' she said. 'I know who he was.'

Elisabeth took the stick from her daughter's mouth. The policeman raised his eyebrows. 'Who?' he asked.

'He was an angel,' Maria said. 'God sent an angel to rescue me.'

'How do you know he was an angel?'

'Because he had wings, silly. Big golden wings.' Maria flapped her arms and laughed. 'I saw him land right by the car. He came out of the sky.'

20

Baywatch

BLANC-SABLON, LABRADOR, CANADA, 1990

Philip Salice was waiting for the boat to take him across the Strait of Belle Isle from Blanc Sablon to St Barbe in Newfoundland. It was late fall and he was cold. The chill in the morning air made him shiver and it crossed his mind that maybe a man of his age should not be making these trips.

He was sixty and for the past thirty years had fished and hunted in this sub-arctic wilderness on the north-eastern edge of the Canadian Shield. He had caught many things here but never a cold. Labrador was desolate and dangerous, but Salice called it 'home sweet home', even though he lived thousands of miles away in Montreal and only visited the snow-covered wilds for two weeks each year.

It was his escape, and now as he stood watching the mist rolling in over the water he was glad he'd ignored the advice of his doctor: 'Take it easy, Philip; slow down.' *What nonsense*, he thought. *There's nothing wrong with me; I'm fighting fit.* But as he watched the motor launch come alongside the wooden pier he felt another sharp pain in his chest; the pain his doctor had warned him not to ignore; the pain that was becoming more frequent and more intense.

'Good morning, Mr Salice,' the skipper of the boat greeted him. 'Always the adventurer! You don't change, do you? Why not catch the ferry for a change? The crossing is not as rough and a man of your age should be careful.'

'Don't you start,' Salice snapped. 'I'm not that much older than you. Anyway, I've always crossed the Strait in your boat. It's quicker, and I used to appreciate the company – until today.' He gave the skipper a mock frown, then smiled. 'My doctor thinks I should be at home with my feet up. What do you think?'

'I will tell you after you give me the twenty dollars for the crossing,' came the reply. 'Come on, old man, get in before I change my mind.' The skipper laughed and helped Salice load his gear into the boat.

It started to rain, a slow, heavy rain, but Salice would not shelter below deck. He wanted to see the icebergs floating down the Strait from Greenland and watch the minke and humpback whales break the surface of the icy water. He loved crossing the Strait, always had, always would, and he stood up to stretch.

Suddenly the pain returned, but this time it was much worse. It felt as though a burning stake was being driven into his chest. His whole body convulsed, his legs buckled. When he hit the icy water his right hand was still clutched to his chest.

By the time the skipper realised what had happened and turned the boat around Salice was nowhere to be seen. Men much younger and stronger had perished in the sub-arctic swell, frozen to death, hearts stopped dead by the shock. Salice had no chance, and the skipper cried as he searched.

A crowd had gathered on the rocks by the side of the water. A doctor was kneeling, examining the body. The onlookers were silent, not daring even to whisper. But when the doctor helped the drenched, shivering man sit up against a rock, the crowd sighed, a deep, grateful sigh. He was alive. Philip Salice was alive.

The skipper could not believe it when he heard the news. 'Are you sure?' he asked, as he walked briskly down the wooden pier. 'It's impossible, absolutely impossible. Philip Salice fell overboard.

I think he had a heart attack on the boat. He can't be alive. We were over a mile out.'

The man who had waited for the skipper was now trying to keep up with him as he ran toward the house where Salice had been taken. 'I'm not sure how he got back to shore,' the man said, gasping. 'I heard something about someone saving him.'

The skipper found Salice sitting in a chair by a log fire. He walked straight over, knelt down and threw his arms around him. 'Thank God, thank God,' he said. 'But I don't understand; I thought you were dead.'

Salice smiled. 'So did I. The doctor here says I ought to be!' He sipped hot coffee from a mug. 'I don't remember much. I felt pain in my chest and was gasping for air when the freezing water hit me. I must have blacked out then because the next thing I see is people standing on the shore, and this big guy towering above me, carrying me out of the water.'

The skipper turned to the doctor, his curiosity aroused.

'A couple of people saw it,' the doctor confirmed. 'They saw a big man towing Mr Salice through the water, then he carried him to the rocks.'

'Who is he? Where is he now?' the skipper wanted to know. He looked confused and a little shaken.

'He disappeared,' Salice said.

The skipper shook his head. 'I'm sorry,' he said. 'I don't doubt what you say is true, because you are alive and someone must have saved you. But where did this guy come from? What was he doing in the middle of the Strait? There were no other boats about, and he sure as hell wasn't swimming out there.'

Salice looked across at the doctor. 'Tell him about the girl.'

'What girl? What are you talking about?' the skipper demanded.

'Keep your voice down, please,' the doctor urged him.

'Look,' said the skipper angrily. 'I think I'm entitled to be a little upset. You don't understand what I've just been through.'

Salice laughed. 'Not as much as I have, but I understand what you must be feeling. Sit down and I'll tell you about the girl.'

The skipper was in no mood to sit. 'Go on,' he said.

Salice cleared his throat. 'Well, a young girl called the doctor on the phone to say she had been looking through her telescope watching a boat cross the Strait. She says she saw me fall overboard. But she tells the doctor not to worry because she had already asked God to send an angel to save me.'

The skipper's eyes couldn't have opened any wider. 'An *angel*?'

Salice smiled, nodding, then coughed before he went on: 'The girl just told the doctor to be on the shore by the rocks.'

'It's true,' said the doctor, 'but I didn't believe her. I knew who she was, I recognised her voice; she's the daughter of one of my patients, a sensible, honest girl. She does like to watch boats through her father's telescope. I knew she would be telling the truth about seeing someone fall overboard. I just presumed whoever they were must surely have drowned in that freezing water.'

'It's a miracle,' Salice said with a smile. 'The doctor can't find anything wrong with me – can you?'

The doctor shook his head. 'No, you are fine. There's nothing to suggest you suffered a heart attack, no sign of hypothermia, no problems at all. It's incredible, but you're in pretty good shape.'

Salice beamed at the skipper. 'How about that for an old man?'

21

Message in a Bottle

AUCKLAND, NEW ZEALAND, 1995

Emma and John Mackay have a good marriage now, and can see a bright future together. Emma wants to start a family. She reckons John would make a good father. He has the joy of rediscovering the woman he married and is determined to do what is right by her. There is passion, commitment and respect in their relationship. It is a marriage with 'made in heaven' stamped all over it, but it never used to be like this. It was, in Emma's own words, 'the marriage from hell'.

In the summer of '92 John Mackay hit rock-bottom. He was an alcoholic and on the night he almost killed Emma he tried to kill himself. She lay in a pool of blood on the kitchen floor of their city apartment. John had come home violently drunk and beat his wife until she passed out. He then took off his belt, hooked the buckle over a skylight-window latch, climbed on to a bar-stool, put the noose around his neck and stepped forward. He hung from the skylight for ten seconds before the latch snapped and he hit the floor unconscious.

Emma came to with a broken nose and smashed jaw, her body bruised and aching. She saw her husband lying face down under the skylight. The belt was still attached to his neck and the broken latch and splinters of wood from the window frame were on the carpet next to him. Emma felt nauseous as she crawled toward the body. A faint pulse told her John was alive, but for one moment she wanted to pull the belt tight around his neck and keep on pulling until the pulse stopped.

'It was the end of the road,' she recalls, 'the lowest point in my life and I really wished John was dead. Deep down I loved him; he was my first love, my true love, and I believe that deep in his heart he still loved me. But after two years of watching him abuse himself and our love with drink, I couldn't take any more. I began to hate him, to detest what he had become, and I made up my mind to leave. I wanted to erase him from my life, for ever.'

John started drinking heavily the day he lost his job. He was a graphic designer, with the same company for eight years, talented but expendable. He took it badly. The timing didn't help; they fired him three days before Christmas 1990, the same date as Emma's twenty-ninth birthday, two days after he hit the big three-o.

'John changed overnight,' Emma recalls. 'It was like "goodbye Dr Jeckyll, hello Mr Hyde." The transformation was frightening. John became a different person. He loved his job, lived for his work, right or wrong, and put his heart and soul into it. When it was taken away from him he just freaked out.'

For the first three months Emma did everything she could to put her husband's shattered world back together. But John gave up living the day he became a dole-queue statistic. He had never been off work for more than a few days at a time in his life but suddenly he had forgotten *how* to work. He became depressed.

'Maybe some guys just take it harder than others,' he says. 'Maybe I had given too much of myself, too much of my soul, to something that, in the greater scheme of things, didn't really count that much. But at the time my work was my whole world, and that world had just caved in. I couldn't see a way-out, and with every week that passed I sank deeper into depression. After a while the only thing that I cared about was my next drink. It was that bad.'

Emma walked out the night John attempted suicide. She went to stay with her parents north of the city. It wasn't the first time John had beaten her, but she was going to make sure it would be the last. 'I just left him lying on the floor,' she recalls. 'I didn't even phone for an ambulance. He was alive and I knew that if I was there when he came round I'd feel sorry for him and end up staying. It sounds crazy, I know, but that's the way it had been for two years.

'He would come home drunk, pick a fight, and hit me. I'd threaten to leave, but in the morning he'd cry and I'd forgive him. I knew he was sick, so I made excuses for him. I knew it wasn't his fault. He tried to stop drinking, tried everything – doctors, clinics, therapy – but he just couldn't stop and it was destroying both our lives. When he tried to kill himself something inside me just snapped. I felt cold, numb, and knew right then that it was over. I couldn't help or reach him any more. He couldn't even help himself. Two years of soul-destroying anger and fear had left me emotionally and physically drained. When I walked out the door that night I honestly believed it was the end for me and John. I could see no way back.'

Two months passed before Emma saw John again. He was lying on a hospital trolley with a stomach pump tube down his throat.

'He hadn't called since I left,' Emma says. 'I'd contacted the couple who lived above our apartment to make sure John was okay. It was a guilt thing, I guess, even though I knew I was the victim. They told me he was fine. I was a little shocked. John had gone up to their apartment the very next day after he'd tried to kill himself and asked for some aspirin. He told them he'd got the worst hangover of his life and, right there and then, vowed to give up drinking.

'He called my parents' home three days later; said he knew

that's where I would be. I wouldn't go to the phone. He told my father he was sorry and that he was determined to sort himself out; said he'd booked himself into a drying out clinic and promised to make it up to me and my parents when he was cured. I didn't believe him. About seven weeks later I got a call from the couple in the apartment upstairs. John had tried to kill himself again, this time with whiskey and sleeping tablets.'

Two weeks later Emma moved John into her parents' home. 'It was against my better judgment,' she says, 'but he was in a mess and my mother somehow convinced me it was my duty as his wife to be there for him. There was no way I was going to move back into the apartment, so I agreed to allow John to move into my mum and dad's place. I figured it would be for just a couple of weeks, until he got back on his feet and started drinking again. The psychiatrist who examined John after he'd tried to kill himself the second time thought staying with family was a good idea. He believed that, with support, John was capable of kicking his habit. I didn't.'

Emma's mother, Christina McPherson, had not stopped praying for her daughter and son-in-law since John had lost his job. The week before John had overdosed she'd given Emma a copy of her favourite book, Smith Wigglesworth's *Ever-Increasing Faith*. 'God heals alcoholics just like he heals the blind and lame,' she told Emma. 'John is sick but there is a cure in the Lord. Read this, and then we'll pray.'

Emma had accepted the book with some reluctance. 'What's this, my last hope?' she'd said. 'You know I don't believe in all this Christian stuff.'

Christina had smiled and put her arms around her daughter. 'I believe that deep down you know that Jesus is the answer. He loves you and John and, frankly, he is your only hope. Just read the pages I've marked, dear. Jesus can do the same for John as he did for the man in the story.'

Emma had opened the book and read:

'A woman came to me in the city of Liverpool and said, "I would like you to help me. I wish you would join me in prayer. My husband is a drunkard and every night comes into the home under the influence of drink. Won't you join me in prayer for him?" I said to the woman, "Have you a handkerchief?" She took out a handkerchief and I prayed over it and told her to lay it on the pillow of the drunken man. He came home that night and laid his head on the pillow in which this handkerchief was tucked. He laid his head on more than the pillow that night. He laid his head on the promise of God. In Mark 11:24, we read, "What things soever ye desire when ye pray, believe that ye receive them, and ye shall have them."

'The next morning the man got up and stopped at the first saloon that he had to pass on his way to work and ordered some beer. He tasted it and said to the bartender, "You have put some poison in this beer." He could not drink it and went on to the next saloon and ordered some more beer. He tasted it and said to the man behind the counter, "You have put some poison in this beer; I believe you folks have agreed to poison me." The bartender was indignant. The man said, "I will go somewhere else." He went to another saloon and the same thing happened as in the two previous saloons. He made such a fuss that they turned him out. After he got off work he went to another saloon to get some beer, and again he thought he had been poisoned; he made so much disturbance that he was thrown out. He went to his home and told his wife what had happened and said: "It seems as though all the fellows have agreed to poison me." His wife said to him, "Can't you see the hand of the Lord in this, that He is making you dislike the stuff that has been your ruin?" This word brought conviction to the man's heart, and he came to the meeting and got saved. The Lord has power to set the captives free.'

By the time John arrived at the McPhersons' place Emma had read the story several times. 'I could not stop thinking about it,' she recalls. 'At first I dismissed it out of hand, but then John overdosed and I got scared. Seeing him lying in that hospital bed, looking more like sixty-one than thirty-one, really hurt. I felt his pain and remembered what Mum had said, that Jesus was the only hope. I could have walked away – all the pain he'd inflicted on me was reason enough to leave him to face his problems alone – but I couldn't stop thinking about that story. I wondered what would have happened if that woman had *not* believed God for her husband's salvation. Would he have ended up a dead drunk, lying in some gutter somewhere, or taking his own life because he couldn't stand what he had become? I guess deep down I loved John too much to abandon him, and something inside of me started to believe in miracles.'

Christina asked her church for help. They agreed to join with her in prayer for John and the day before he arrived at the house the McPhersons and the pastor of the church prayed over a handkerchief. Christina gave it to Emma and she tucked it inside the pillow on the bed where John was to lie. His appearance had shocked Emma's parents. He did look twice his age, gaunt and jaundiced, and was so weak he could hardly walk. Emma and her father, Josh, had to help him out of the car and up the stairs to the bedroom.

John slept for fifteen hours. Then he awoke suddenly and sat bolt upright in bed. He didn't know it at the time, but he was a changed man.

John thought he must be dreaming still because his body felt warm after being bathed in heavenly light for what seemed an eternity. Moments passed and he began to adjust to his surroundings. He looked at the brass alarm clock on the dresser by the bed. It was midday and he could hear the spatter of rain on the windows. *Weird*, he thought. *Something's not right*. But he could not put his finger on what was wrong.

The dream had been so vivid, so real. In it he had been wandering, dying of thirst, in a desolate place, a barren, rock-strewn landscape, when an angel appeared on the path ahead. He was tall; a giant, winged being, dressed in golden robes with long, flowing silver hair. He spoke in a gentle, authoritative voice. 'Jesus is waiting for you,' said the angel, pointing toward an oasis of green trees and blue water in the distance. 'He is the Lord of Lords and the King of Kings. He is the Son of God. He longs to fellowship with you, John. Go now, go to be with your Saviour.'

John turned to look at the oasis. It was not far away and yet he had not seen it before. When he turned back the angel had gone. John blinked in the scorching sun, and then the oasis was gone. He found himself walking by the side of a stream. He was knee-deep in lush grass, with trees overhanging the water, fanned by a cool breeze. Wild flowers of many colours stretched across the meadow as far as the eye could see, like a rainbow springing from the earth. He followed these colours with an urgency, a desire he could not understand. He was almost breaking into a run as he made his way toward a thicket in the far corner of the meadow, where the wild flowers swept out and upward in a multicoloured carpet across the point on the horizon where the grass touched the sky.

He was running now, the long grass swishing on his legs. With every stride he grew stronger, the ground beneath his feet absorbing and replenishing the spring in his step. His heart was beating quickly, in vibrant rhythm, as he approached the trees. He stopped running before he reached the edge of what he could now see was an orchard of at least fifty trees, their branches weighed down with fruit and almost touching the ground. The sweet perfume of nectar filled the air. John breathed in, slowly and deeply, and closed his eyes. All at once, before he could open them again, a surge of power – supernatural energy – coursed through his body. He knew he was not alone. An awesome, holy presence permeated the atmosphere. John slowly opened his eyes and a radiant, soul-penetrating light flooded his being and he felt his spirit soar. And then, ahead of him, he saw the Son of God, Jesus Christ, holding out his hand in welcome. John fell upon his knees and cried tears of joy.

John had been healed, miraculously healed. One week after Emma had tucked the handkerchief into his pillow John's face was still glowing. 'You look as though you've just come back from a holiday in the sun,' Josh told him. 'God has blessed you, John. You've had a touch from the Lord.'

John knew it. He looked and felt younger than thirty-one. He had lost his taste for alcohol. For the first time in more than two years he had no craving, no manic depression. Gone, too, were the terrible aches and pains he had suffered. He recalled his life before the night of the dream but had difficulty remembering what it was like. His memory had not been erased, but the consuming agony in his heart had disappeared. He felt born again.

Emma had never known such joy. As the weeks and months passed she watched John grow stronger and stronger in God. She told him of the pain he had inflicted on her and how she had wanted him to die. John listened and held her tenderly when she cried. He asked her for forgiveness and she gave it.

One spring morning they went to church where they re-dedicated their lives to each other, and to God.

The 'marriage from hell' had been touched by heaven.

22

Lifeblood

NEAR LONDON, ENGLAND, 1994

By the end of 1989 young Sam Mildenburger had been given up for dead. Less than a year old when an incurable blood disorder was diagnosed, his body was wasting away and his broken-hearted parents were steeling themselves for the worst. The doctors had explained that Sam's condition – familial erythropharylic lympho histocytosis – was very rare, and that for a child to survive, let alone make a complete recovery, was rarer still.

But today Sam confounds the medical experts, and the only concern his parents have is how to keep up with their bouncing boy whose zest for life no doubt springs from the fact that he nearly didn't have one.

News of Sam's condition was first broken to Marian and Alan Mildenburger in July 1989. Chemotherapy treatment and an experimental bone-marrow transplant failed and by Christmas there was nothing else doctors could offer. They had given up hope.

'My whole life collapsed,' Marian recalls. 'In desperation, I turned to prayer, with no great faith, I have to admit, but with God's help we were put in touch with a church where everyone was so friendly and helpful. The pastor went and prayed for Sam, and his condition, which doctors had said could only deteriorate, stabilised.'

But in April 1990 Sam's condition took a turn for the worse. His stomach swelled up, his liver and kidneys ceased to function properly, and his heart expanded. By the time the fits started Sam's blood pressure was so high that the doctors said he could not survive. If he started to slip away, they said, there was no point in trying to save him.

Again the pastor prayed, this time raising a few medical eyebrows as he stormed into the boy's hospital room, shouting to Sam that he was not to be afraid because Jesus was 'punching it through with him'. To the doctors' amazement, Sam regained consciousness, and within twenty-four hours was sitting up in his cot playing with his toys.

At the time Sam left hospital the platelet count in his blood was around 9,000 per cubic millilitre, as opposed to 150,000–500,000 for a normal child. At one point he needed three platelet transfusions a week, and doctors said they would continue. Yet at the time of writing he has not needed a transfusion for four years and his immune system is working normally. Doctors also predicted that Sam would suffer permanent brain damage as a consequence of the disease and of the treatment he received. In 1991 a scan revealed areas of calcification in the brain which suggested they were right. Three years later, however, there was no trace of any abnormality.

When Sam reached four years of age an educational psychologist ran a battery of tests on him and found that in every way he was equal with his age group. After his fifth birthday he joined his sister at school for the first time and loved it. 'It was wonderful to see him joining in the rough and tumble of school life,' Marian says. 'What's happened to him is marvellous; even doctors beam with delight and amazement that he is alive and able to run, ride a bike, and do all the things that normal, healthy kids do.'

Tests conducted in 1994 revealed that Sam Mildenburger's

recovery cannot be attributed to the compatible bone marrow transplant attempted by doctors in 1989 using bone marrow donated by Alan Mildenburger. DNA tests have shown that all his cells still have his own DNA pattern.

What does that mean in layman's terms? As his plain-speaking doctors will tell you: 'Sam Mildenburger – he's a walking miracle.'

23

Church on Fire

LUTON, ENGLAND, 1969

The Reverend Colin Urquhart didn't know what he was letting himself in for. He had just agreed to become the vicar of a church with a bad reputation; a post that had already broken two men. 'It's a tough job,' the Bishop said. 'The first priest had a nervous breakdown and the present vicar's health has just given way under the strain. There will be a lot of hard work, and it's no use expecting much response. So we would only leave you there five years: you'll have had enough by then.'

Some prospect, thought Colin, and doubts started to dog him. Did God really want him at St Hugh's, Lewsey? Maybe there was a whole lot of trouble just waiting to explode in his face the minute he showed up on that sprawling housing estate. Maybe he'd experience the same fate as the priest and the vicar. The only thing he could be sure of was that his faith was about to be tested.

What Colin didn't know – and what he may have found more daunting even than St Hugh's troubled history – was that God had big plans for the church. These plans began to unfold in a movement of the Holy Spirit that is now known as 'charismatic renewal'. Within four years the church with the bad reputation had changed beyond recognition as God touched people's lives, bringing healing and restored relationships to all areas where there was lack. In body and mind, in relationships, in business, God moved with power. And even now, more than twenty years later, people still talk with excitement about those days of divine visitation.

It was April 1970 when Colin and his wife Caroline moved with their children to Lewsey. Four weeks earlier, Andrea, their third child, was born with what is commonly called 'clicky hips'. The lining of her hip joints was imperfectly formed, causing the bones to click. She was put in a frame which kept her legs apart and prevented the hip joints from moving freely. It was hoped that over a period of a few weeks the defect would be rectified.

Three weeks after the birth Caroline took the baby to see the consultant. He shook his head sadly. 'I'm afraid there are no signs of improvement,' he said. 'Her movement will be impaired until she is eighteen months old. She will then have surgery and will be in plaster for some time. After that she will need calipers, and will have to learn to walk.'

'My wife was in tears when she got back from the hospital,' Colin recalls. 'There was only one thing for it: prayer. The following week, only a day or two before our move, the consultant examined Andrea again, very thoroughly. "She seems to be fine," he said, "she doesn't need that frame any more." We knew God had healed her.'

St Hugh's was a new parish. The church building was only three years old when Colin arrived, and by the time it was consecrated every penny of its cost had been repaid. A congregation of loyal communicants had worked hard to establish the church in this new area, but there was discontent among the faithful. 'Is this what it's all about, raising money for new buildings, then having stewardship campaigns to support them?'

'No,' Colin answered, 'it's not all.'

'Then what else is there?'

'Just wait and see,' he said, believing they were about to set out on a great adventure together.

'None of us knew where we were going or what the journey would be like,' he says. 'Deep within was the conviction that it was going to be different from anything I had known. God himself was very definitely going to be in charge. My first sermon was about Jesus walking on the water, and we were soon to discover that it is exhilarating "walking on the water" with Jesus.'

Within a matter of weeks prayer and healing groups were established. People were eager to learn how to pray, with nearly a hundred pledging to become members. It wasn't long before miraculous healings began.

Stella, a schoolteacher and a leading member of the church council, was one of the first to be touched. Ever since the birth of her second daughter, Gillian, fourteen years earlier, she had suffered from a very uncomfortable and medically incurable kidney complaint. 'You will have to learn to live with the pain,' she had been told by her doctor.

But Stella was given the faith to believe that God could heal her, and the church agreed to meet for prayer one day after school. When Colin met her in the church he said to her: 'Well, Stella, it's going to happen, isn't it?'

'Yes,' she replied, 'it is. I know it is. God is going to heal me.'

They prayed together, praising God for all his love and goodness. Colin laid hands on Stella and prayed that God would heal her.

'She looked radiant,' he recalls, 'and just began thanking God. Apart from the kidney disease, Stella was suffering from arthritis in the neck and rheumatic pains in different parts of her body. As she praised, the discomfort began to disappear.'

'Oh, thank you, thank you, God.' She was weeping tears of joy. 'Thank you, thank you.'

'What about the kidneys?' Colin asked.

'Only time will prove that they are healed,' Stella said, 'but I know they are, I just know it.'

'Stella was healed not only of her aches and pains, but of the kidney disease as well,' Colin recalls. 'Time has proved that. Her healing was a cause of great rejoicing and encouragement to all who were beginning to pray.'

Norma had been suffering with rheumatoid arthritis for eight years. It had affected nearly every joint in her body, causing pain and stiffness. She had two slipped discs and a virus infection in her spinal fluid, which was affecting her central nervous system. She also had a growth on her spine. Colin asked Norma what hope she had been given by her doctors.

'I've been told that within six months I'll be in a wheelchair,' she replied, 'and that I'll stay in it for the rest of my life.' This grim prognosis had driven Norma to decide that suicide would be preferable to becoming a burden to her husband and school-aged children.

Sensing the situation was desperate, Colin set about explaining to Norma how God could give her the faith to believe that she would be healed. 'She looked unbelieving at first,' he recalls, 'but what I was saying offered some hope and eventually she was longing to lay her whole life before God. We prayed and she was filled with praise. I was becoming accustomed to seeing people's lives change, but something out of the ordinary was happening to Norma.

'We didn't pray for physical healing immediately. It was when we met again that we prayed that God would heal the disease which was causing paralysis and pain in her body. There was no instant miracle. During the course of the next few months we prayed twice, sometimes three times, each week, and I saw God do some remarkable things to Norma during that time.'

Colin is convinced God performed a kind of physiotherapy, releasing the joints from stiffness and pain. First, the neck was freed, then the shoulders and arms, the hips and then the legs. Six months passed and, instead of being confined to a wheelchair, Norma was caring for her family and holding down a part-time job as well. 'I remember laying hands on Norma's back and feeling the locked joints begin to move beneath my hands,' he says. 'On another occasion, one of her fingers was healed. The knuckle joint had disappeared and the finger could not be bent. As we prayed she began to move the finger. At first there was a slight crackling noise, but this stopped when the joint was completely freed. The finger looked as good as new.'

During Norma's regular hospital visits the doctors would check on the rate that paralysis was spreading and her limbs were stiffening. Now they could not understand what was happening; as far as they were concerned it should have been impossible for her to walk.

'She was asked to spend a few days in hospital, so that tests could be carried out,' Colin says. 'She didn't want to do this because she knew God was healing her. She was subjected to a whole series of examinations, and the doctors could not believe the results of their tests.'

One morning she was given yet another examination. 'Would you mind telling me what's going on?' she asked. 'So many doctors have examined me and nobody will tell me why.'

'I can't say anything,' she was told. 'I'm not your doctor. It's amazing, unbelievable. You are a very interesting case.'

Norma was afraid. The secrecy of those continual examinations was making her think that perhaps her healing was an illusion and that the medical evidence did not substantiate it.

'But her fears were groundless. Her body showed no signs of the serious spinal infection, and the rheumatoid arthritis had disappeared. The doctors asked Norma's permission to operate on the growth on her spine, but she refused. In her heart, she knew that God was healing her.'

She was discharged on the condition that she returned for further examinations, and the healing progressed until there was only one small area of pain toward the base of the spine.

'This stubbornly refused to move,' said Colin. 'I could not understand why the pain was persisting and asked God, "What do I do now?" The answer came like a thunderbolt from the blue: "Address the evil." But how? I did not know. I simply said: "I address you, power of evil, and in the name of Jesus, I command you to go."'

There was an immediate reaction within Norma, as if some latent entity had been stirred. Suddenly she was being choked and felt physically sick. This struggle lasted for a few minutes and was followed by peace. When Norma returned to hospital she was told by the consultant that no operation would be necessary. She was discharged.

Perhaps the most remarkable healing that took place at St Hugh's concerned a two-year-old boy called David. He was almost a human vegetable; he could not stand or walk. He sat on the floor all day long, with a totally blank expression on his face, unable to hear and hardly able to see. The amount of brain damage left no hope of David ever improving through medical treatment.

'His family had only just moved into the district when Shirley, his mother, fell into conversation with two other women who lived in the same street, Maggie and Tina, both members of St Hugh's,' Colin recollects. 'When Shirley told them about David they said that they would pray for him at their healing group. Immediately David began to change. Within two weeks he was not only standing, he was running. And he could hear, and was beginning to talk. The blank expression had gone; instead he was laughing and even singing.'

Shirley was accused of bringing the wrong child when she next visited the clinic! 'That cannot possibly be the child referred to in these notes,' she was told. The health visitor said that in all her experience she had never known any child to be healed of such advanced brain damage.

The congregation was well into Wesley's spirited hymn, 'O, for a thousand tongues to sing' when Colin heard a trumpet playing. He didn't take much notice at first. John, a member of St Hugh's, would often accompany the organ on his trumpet, but when Colin looked toward the back of the church expecting to see him, he was not there.

'I listened more intently and realised that I could hear not one trumpet, but several,' Colin says. 'They were blending beautifully with the organ. I was so certain that this was not my imagination that, when the hymn ended, I said to everyone: "I heard trumpets during that hymn." Several people nodded and after the service confirmed that they too had heard the heavenly trumpets.

'Later, Stewart, our organist, said to me: "Something strange happened to the organ; the trumpet stop refused to work during that hymn. It was working perfectly up until then; it worked perfectly afterwards, but it would not work at all during that hymn."'

In May 1973, three years after Colin arrived in Lewsey, someone tried to burn St Hugh's to the ground. Close to midnight they lit three fires: one on the altar, one on a table, and the other among a pile of books near the entrance. Early the following morning Colin went into church to prepare for Holy Communion and was met by a thick wall of smoke. He could see flames just inside the door and hear crackling noises coming from the direction of the altar at the other end of the building. The smoke was so dense that he could only take a few steps before being driven back, so he rang for the fire brigade.

They soon arrived and put out the fire. The fire chief stood in the church and shook his head in disbelief. He had examined the charred wood at one corner of the altar and confirmed that the fire had definitely been burning all night. 'I cannot understand,' he said, 'why the whole place did not go up in flames. A building with this volume of air should have burned easily.'

'I don't think he would have accepted our explanation,' Colin says with a smile. 'It was another wondrous miracle.'

24

Walking on Air

THE HAGUE, HOLLAND, 1993

Dr Jacques Ewals could not believe what he was seeing. It was as though the woman before him had been given a new body. During a lifetime in medicine he had never come across such a thing: a supernatural transformation.

He was looking at someone who had been crippled and wasted with a painful, incurable muscular disease. And yet as he examined Helen de Jong he could find no sign of the malady. The doctor was convinced his patient had received a miracle cure.

'There is no other explanation,' said Jacques Ewals, a consultant rheumatologist at the Rode Kruis Hospital. 'Mrs de Jong was suffering severe muscular and joint pain; her body was covered in what is clinically called "tender spots"; and she had severe fatigue. There is no medical treatment for the condition known as fibromyalgia, but when I saw her she was totally free of any symptoms.'

Helen de Jong was desperate when she decided to attend a church meeting. Doctors had attempted to slow the process of the disease but it had developed rapidly and Helen had become a prisoner in the home she shared with her husband and five children.

'They told me there was no cure, no escape for me,' she recalls, 'and I realised that it was going to be very much a case of living for today; I would have gone out of my mind if I'd dwelt too much on the future.

'I'd always believed that God could heal, although I did not think about the possibility of a miracle for myself. But when the pastor placed his hands on me the pain instantly disappeared. I was so excited at the time, I didn't realise the crippling tiredness had vanished too. God healed me, just like that, and I was suddenly walking on air. I felt like a little child who had received a special present.

'For days, I was on cloud nine. It took a long time for what God had done to sink in. It was wonderful being able to do things again; things which had been impossible before were now easy. Even little things like doing the housework meant a lot to me after so many months. God seemed close to me in a new way; with my physical healing came spiritual healing, too. God took away all the feelings of sorrow, suffering and hurt, and a great peace came inside.'

Jacques Ewals knew he was looking at a walking miracle. 'I was utterly amazed that she was free of the disease in such a short time,' he said. 'It was only a matter of weeks after Mrs de Jong attended church, but she had made a complete recovery. The disease had gone. The healing suggests that miracles still exist in this world.'

25

Too Young to Die

ITALY, 1994

The people standing around the body of the baby were in deep shock. They had seen the tiny girl fall from a fourth floor window; heard the awful impact as she struck the concrete floor below; felt sick when they saw no sign of life. But they cried with joy as she was raised from the dead.

It was all over in less than five minutes, but they will remember the moment for the rest of their lives, maybe longer. It happened in a small fishing town close to the Adriatic city of Pescara. The tiny girl's name is Gabrielle. She was fifteen months old when she fell from the window. Her six-year-old brother Roberto says she was too young to die, so God saved her.

It was that simple, according to Roberto, who remembered what he had learned in Sunday school at the Christian mission and put it into practice when Gabrielle fell thirty feet, head first.

She had toddled into the bathroom, climbed on to the window-shelf, unhooked the catch, and fallen out.

Roberto was kicking a football on the pavement below and saw Gabrielle fall. For a moment he froze, not knowing what to do. Then he recalled the story of how Jesus raised Lazarus from the dead, and prayed: 'I believe You can do it again, I really do.'

Roberto ran over to where his sister's broken body lay. He saw his mother kneeling over Gabrielle. He heard her screaming.

Another woman was trying to tell her the child was dead; that it was no use trying to shake her back to life.

The boy took no notice. His mother saw him coming through the crowd and tried to keep him away, but before she could grab him, Roberto bent over Gabrielle, placing his hands on her head, and shouted: 'Get up, Gabby. Jesus says you are too young to die.'

Suddenly the girl's legs twitched, then her head moved. The mother screamed again.

'Told you so,' Roberto said, and went back to his football.

By the time the ambulance arrived, Gabrielle was on her feet. 'It's a miracle,' the mother said. 'She was dead, there was no pulse, no sign of life. But look at her now; she is fine.'

At the hospital doctors shook their heads in amazement. 'How far did she fall?' they asked. 'Are you sure? Was it really concrete she landed on?'

'Yes, yes, it really happened, and you are right to doubt because my baby should be dead,' the mother replied. 'She is so tiny and fragile and would not have survived, had a miracle not taken place.'

'We do not believe in such things,' one of the doctors said, 'but there is no logical explanation for what happened to your daughter today. She is just lucky to be alive.'

'It has nothing to do with luck.' The mother had tears in her eyes. 'Just a small boy's faith in God, and God's love for his children.'

26

Steps of Faith

ENGLAND, 1989

Something was killing Julie Sheldon, something horrific. It came from nowhere; a vicious, uncontrollable attack, raging inside her body, rampant and destructive. Toward the end, when doctors had given up hope and the dark shadow of death appeared, her body was hideously contorted. Both legs drawn up; arms at right angles, one hand in a claw, the other a fist; head pulled to one side.

Ferocious convulsions forced her legs to retract even farther and tangle together; her arms to twist and bend behind her back; her head to snap right back, arching the spine until she started to choke, strangled and suffocated by her own muscles. And there was nothing she could do to stop this awful thing; she was conscious, but paralysed by fearful pain. Trapped inside a self-destructing body, Julie believed she was going to die.

'It all started so innocently, so undramatically,' she writes in her autobiography, *Dancer off her Feet* — long before the doctors diagnosed dystonia, the crippling, life-threatening neurological disease caused by abnormal brain functions; and long after she danced with Nureyev and Fonteyn in the Royal Ballet. Somewhere between the good times and the worst of times, between the light and the darkness, it started. No warning, just a strange, uneasy feeling.

And yet, when the truth was known, Julie wasn't frightened. Deep inside she knew that pain and disease were going to be with her for some time to come; that 'some great, extraordinary plan was beginning to unfold', in which she had to play her part. And even when the illness threatened to kill her, she hung on to a strong belief that nothing in all creation could separate her from the love of God; a belief that God would not forsake her; that he would mend her twisted body and heal her mind and spirit.

For three years she believed this, her life hanging in the balance. And then, one day, she was completely healed. Hundreds, maybe thousands, of prayers, carried on the wings of faith, hope and love, were answered.

Julie's story began to go wrong in 1973. She was fourteen and an exceptionally talented ballet dancer 'chasing the dream of a lifetime': a place in the Royal Ballet School. Hundreds of dancers from all over the world were competing against one another for only sixteen places. Julie was destined to become one of the élite. But dark demons were already gathering in the wings. Julie's ballet mistress had spotted a small tilt in her posture – a 'tilt' which the orthopaedic consultant diagnosed as curvature of the spine. 'If you carry on with your training as a ballet dancer,' he told her, 'you will be confined to a wheelchair by the time you are thirty.'

Julie reeled in horror. *There must be some mistake*, she thought. She was not in pain and the small abnormality did not affect her dancing. But the consultant was adamant. There was a serious weakness in Julie's back, and it was too dangerous to aggravate.

'It was a very difficult decision for my parents,' she says. 'They knew dancing was my whole world. In the end we shelved any decision. As long as it was causing no real problem we might as well carry on. Besides, I was determined that nothing would stop me reaching the top. But I never dreamt how prophetic the doctor's words would be.'

Next, a cystic swelling on the tendon of Julie's wrist had to be operated on. Then stomach-ache turned into acute appendicitis, and following surgery the wound became infected and developed an abscess. For nine weeks the fever raged, but when it began to subside disaster struck again. Julie almost fractured her skull falling down a flight of stairs. It was weeks before she was able to dance properly again. And all the while, the doctor's prediction was ticking like a time bomb in the back of her mind.

Julie refused to concede defeat and through sheer determination earned selection to audition for a place at the Royal Ballet School.

'I was thrilled to pass the first round,' she recalls. 'Now only a medical stood between me and the chance of a lifetime. We were checked over like racehorses. Our legs, arms, backs were measured, and our limbs pulled around and over our heads. The spine was carefully examined, and the curve in mine was noted but finally dismissed. I could hardly contain my excitement when I was told I had passed and would be offered a place in the Royal Ballet School in the summer of 1974. The tide of bad luck seemed to have turned.'

But it had only ebbed. Like the dark, foreboding swell of a riptide, the undercurrent of tribulation in Julie's life was churning. A tidal wave was building. And things continued to go wrong. During the first year as a raw sixteen-year-old, while rehearsing in a pas-de-deux class, her partner's hands slipped and she crashed heavily, awkwardly to the floor. 'Sharp pain flashed through my back and for a moment I couldn't move,' she says. 'A check-up by the Royal Ballet doctor revealed nothing serious, so after a couple of days' rest I started classes once more.

'Every movement was an effort, and the pain in my back increased. But looming ahead was the Advanced RAD exam and I had been chosen to dance with Rudolph Nureyev and Dame Margot Fonteyn in the Royal Gala Performance in front of the Queen Mother at Covent Garden. I would not have missed that for the world. It was a marvellous experience, but reality, like the pain in my back, reasserted itself and I was taken to see a Harley Street specialist.'

The diagnosis was not good: a fracture of the fifth lumbar vertebra, aggravated over a seven-month period, causing possible nerve and muscle damage. Julie was clamped into a full body plaster jacket weighing twenty-one pounds and warned not to exercise for at least three months.

'I was heartbroken,' she says. 'To miss three months of ballet at this crucial stage would mean a loss of fitness and concentration which might never be recovered. And I wondered if my back would ever again be strong enough for the demands of a full-time professional career.'

After four months the plaster jacket was removed and Julie returned to ballet training. But something was drastically wrong.

'In my heart I was facing up to a bleak reality. Something was lost, whether it was strength, co-ordination or suppleness, I was not quite sure. Despite working and working until I could hardly stand from exhaustion, I was having to admit that I would never be the prima ballerina I had always dreamt of.'

She left the Royal Ballet School and joined a small ballet company which opened with a production of *Les Sylphides* at the Brighton Dome. But her new career as a professional ballerina lasted only a few weeks. The company had to fold through lack of funds. So, at the age of eighteen, Julie left the country, taking a job as a nanny with a family in Brussels and teaching dancing to children in her spare time.

On her return to England Julie set up a commercial promotions and modelling company called Two's Company, going into business with an American dancer named Catherine, a close friend from her Royal Ballet School days. At the same time Julie's sister Annie was badgering her to go to Motcombe, a Christian holiday retreat in Dorset.

'I could not imagine anything more boring,' she recalls, 'and I was embarrassed, even ashamed, to think about God too much. Faith had played such an important part in our family during my childhood that I was quite aware he could hardly be pleased with my current lifestyle. My social life in London was a million worlds away from that sort of scene.

'But Annie, who had made a conscious decision to commit her life to God, refused to go to Motcombe if I did not go with her, so I gave in. I loathed it. Compared with the exciting "adult" life I was living in London, it seemed like going back to kindergarten. The only way I could cope was by nipping out into the rhododendrons every couple of hours and having a quick smoke. The girls had prayer meetings every morning before breakfast, and before they went to sleep, they sat on their beds and read their Bibles.

'I felt as different from them as if I had two heads, and yet something got to me. There was an atmosphere of great caring and acceptance, and somehow the glittering, flamboyant life in London began to seem hollow and pointless, just an illusion of happiness compared with the peace and joy that the crowd at Motcombe had found in God. I could not get away from it, these girls enjoyed being Christians. This relationship with Jesus they talked about seemed to be so real, so exciting, that I knew I had never known him in that personal way.

'"Behold, I stand at the door and knock." I heard a talk on this Bible verse one morning, and I knew then, with a strange quickening of my heart, that Jesus was wanting to come into my life. One night we sang the familiar chorus,

> Turn your eyes upon Jesus.
> Look full in his wonderful face.
> And the things of earth will grow strangely dim
> In the light of his glory and grace.

These were words I had heard many times before, yet that night there was a huge lump in my throat and I could not sing. Slipping out on to the balcony at the end of the dormitory, I gazed up into the clear starlit night. There seemed to be no one else in the world in that stillness, just God and I meeting at the very centre of creation. Nothing else mattered except that Jesus had loved me enough to die for me, and wanted to share his life with me. "Yes, Jesus," I whispered into the night, "please come in." Out of the heavens his love swept into my heart and I realised without a doubt that Jesus was now my own King and Saviour.'

Julie didn't say much to Catherine. 'I don't know if I could have described to her just what had happened,' she says. Soon Julie saw God at work in her life. Two's Company was enjoying considerable success, winning a contract to help promote Warner Brothers' *Superman*; Julie danced at the opening ceremony of the BAFTA Film Awards in 1979. Then she met Tom, and a storybook romance unfolded. On the morning of her twenty-first birthday he asked for her hand in marriage. Julie could not have been happier as she walked down the aisle. She couldn't possibly have known about what lay ahead. The doctor's prediction was still ticking like a time bomb, but it was now buried under layers of good time; time that had dispelled fears; time that had healed heartache.

'I loved being married,' she says. 'We were having a good time, but suddenly it all came to an abrupt halt. It was approaching Christmas and Tom and I got food poisoning. We were very sick. At three in the morning Tom crawled to the phone and called for the doctor. He came out and rather summarily treated us both with a jab in the bottom. I jumped a mile when my injection went in as it sent a fierce pain searing right down my leg. Tom hardly noticed his jab.'

For several days they were ill, but then Tom began to recover. Julie was afflicted by another problem. The injection had not only affected her sciatic nerve but had caused an abscess which grew to the size of a golf ball. She needed surgery to drain the abscess and had to return for a week's traction to try to free the nerve. But the nerve trauma lasted nearly nine months, making walking and sleeping difficult.

'My family were up in arms about the treatment we had received by the doctor on the first night,' she recalls. 'The hospital felt the injection had been carelessly administered. There was an obvious case for legal action, but in the end we let the matter drop. Eventually the sciatic pain disappeared and the abscess healed, then suddenly I was hit by sickness again. But I quickly realised there was no cause for alarm, I was simply pregnant, and our first child, Amelia, was born on 10 August 1982.'

Two and a half years later, in December 1984, disaster struck during a Christmas family skiing holiday in Thyon, Switzerland. Julie had just discovered she was expecting a second child, but on Christmas Eve she fell heavily, damaging three discs in her neck and top back. Medics at the resort managed to get two of the three discs back into place, but during physiotherapy treatment following her return to England a week later, the left side of Julie's neck and shoulders went into spasm; her hand went numb; and she had severe headaches and pain behind her eyes. The pain continued and complications grew.

A Harley Street specialist was consulted and to Julie's relief he cured the problem with several exhausting sessions of intensive manipulation to her neck. But several months later, just weeks before her second child was due, the pain in the back of Julie's head returned and increased until she could hardly move it. 'The pain seemed to have clamped every nerve in my body in a vice,' she says. 'I could barely think or speak. The doctor suspected meningitis and I was rushed to hospital.'

'First they carried out a lumbar puncture and suspected bacterial meningitis, injecting me with all sorts of antibiotics. I tried to resist all these drugs; all I could think about was my unborn baby, and I was terrified that the drugs would harm or even kill it.'

Eventually, viral meningitis was diagnosed and after weeks of rest, as the virus ran its course, Julie began to improve. She was weak and pale and was plagued with awful headaches and a painful intolerance to light. But scans had not revealed anything wrong with the baby and by 2 September 1985 all her worries disappeared. Georgie was born. 'She was small but perfect, and Tom and I took her home to more than the usual family rejoicing. Our difficulties had made us all appreciate one another so much more, and had drawn Tom and me together in a deeper reliance on God.'

Their faith was soon tested. At seven months, Georgie caught a flu-type virus. One of her lungs collapsed and she was being starved of oxygen. For hours she was close to death.

'She looked grey and wax-like,' Julie says, 'until suddenly she opened her big blue eyes wide and smiled at us, her cheeks instantly tinged with a hint of pinkness. From that moment, I resolved to treat every day with my children and husband as a gift, as something so precious, to be infinitely valued. Little did I know that within a few months I would be parted from them for nearly three years.'

It started with a routine cartilage operation in January 1987. It was minor surgery and Julie was told she would be back to normal within two weeks. But after the operation the pain increased and her knee locked rigid. Further surgery was carried out in an attempt to get Julie's leg working again, but complications set in. The skin on her leg looked strangely discoloured and blotchy, and terrible pain seared through her whole leg. Doctors suspected some kind of malfunction of the sympathetic nerve. They could not have been farther from the truth.

They were waiting for the nerves to calm down, hoping for an improvement, when something incredible happened. Julie was sitting in bed, staring out of the window across the garden and rows of rooftops. She felt down. 'When will this pain end?' she asked. 'God, where are you in all this?'

'Suddenly a profound feeling of his presence filled the room and my mind became sharp and clear. With a flash of illumination, I knew this pain and disability were going to be with me for some time to come. I wasn't frightened, for there was an overwhelming sense of God's love and peace flooding over me, and something almost like joy began to well up deep inside. In the half light I reached for my Bible, and it fell open at Revelation. My hands began to tremble as I made out the words: "Do not fear what you are about to suffer. Behold the devil is about to throw some of you into prison, that you may be tested, and for ten days you will have tribulation. Be faithful unto death, and I will give you the crown of life." (Rev. 2:10)

'I didn't tell anyone about this experience,' she says. 'I felt it was too precious, too fragile to share. I didn't want it discussed, analysed, possibly dismissed as a dream. If the prison was simply going to be pain, perhaps I would be able to hide from everyone just how bad it was.'

There was no chance of that. The pain increased until her leg felt so hot she feared the skin would blister. Doctors were mystified. No one seemed to know what was causing the problem, or how to treat it. Julie was admitted to hospital for nerve blocks to stop the pain. The procedure was difficult and dangerous. On one occasion the pressure inside the inflated cuff, used to stop the blood flow into her leg, caused it to explode just after the drug had been given. The chemical flooded through her body and into her brain. Julie feared she would die until an antidote was quickly administered.

But the nerve blocks were working. The pain lessened and she was nearly able to tolerate touch on her skin, and walk short distances without crutches. It was now midsummer and doctors became hopeful of a full recovery. By October Julie was so much better she was able to take a short holiday in Majorca. She was so happy to be able to stroll along the beach and swim in the sea that she hardly noticed the new niggling pain in her hip.

Shortly after returning to England that pain grew worse. By December it was excruciating. Diagnosed first as bursitis, or inflammation of the hip, the condition was now being called migratory algodystrophy. A week before Christmas Julie was readmitted to hospital. Doctors were not sure that algodystrophy was an adequate diagnosis for the extreme pain and increasing disability Julie was experiencing. She could now barely sit up and all they could do to ease her pain was administer morphine injections every few hours. Cortisone injections into her knee and hip were also given, but the pain still grew worse. Things looked very bleak.

The orthopaedic specialist who had been treating Julie gave up. He was bewildered and called in a physician friend. 'He thought the problem was psychosomatic,' Julie recalls. 'He decided a course of intensive physiotherapy and walking was the answer. I was determined not to be labelled depressive or non-cooperative so I summoned every ounce of strength and tried to walk. Pain hit me until I began to shiver and shake, but I refused to give up. Day after day I half-walked, half-crawled down the corridor, often collapsing and being dragged back to my feet by the physio.

'Afterwards they would leave me alone for hours, and my body, aggravated by the stress of movement, would be in agony. It was like being burnt at the stake, tongues of pain licking round my limbs, consuming more and more of me. Despite all my efforts, I was becoming more and more immobile. I didn't dare tell the doctors the injections seemed no longer to make any difference. Then, a few days later, the doctor confessed to giving me placebos, and, since I was not complaining of more pain, they were probably right in assuming my condition was psychologically induced. I was told to pull myself together and admit it was all in the mind. I was at the end of the line.'

A second opinion was called for and one of the world's top neurologists, Professor Marsden, agreed to transfer Julie to the

National Hospital for tests. Electrodes were attached to her scalp; machines were wired to her body. Reactions to light, sound and sensation were measured. Algodystrophy was confirmed, but there was little the hospital could do and she was allowed home. It was the end of February 1988.

By April Julie was convinced that something more sinister than Algodystrophy was taking hold. The way her right foot was turning in and contracting was not a symptom of that disease. A tremor had started in her right leg and she was readmitted to hospital. There was no diagnosis, no prognosis. Manipulation under anaesthetic was suggested in a desperate attempt to straighten out Julie's contorted leg. It was a success, but only lasted as long as the anaesthetic.

After the MUA doctors agreed to put a plaster cast on the leg under general anaesthetic after straightening it out. The theory was that if the brain once got the message that the leg was meant to be straight it would stop sending signals to the muscles to contract. By now Julie's leg was drawn up almost to her chest, occasionally making big jerks and kicks. The operation was a disaster.

As she came round from the anaesthetic, Julie saw a long white thing flashing past her eyes. In horror she realised that it was her leg flailing around uncontrollably and crashing on to the bed. 'Take it off, take it off,' someone was shouting, but Julie grabbed the surgeon's arm.

'Please leave it,' she gasped. 'We can't give up now. It might settle down in a minute.'

But inside the plaster cast violent muscle spasms were trying to draw the leg back into its foetal position. The plaster started to crack and the leg sprang back across Julie's body like a piece of elastic.

Doctors were now certain the problem was neurological, not rheumatological. More tests were called for. Julie was strapped into a special chair, and wired up to hundreds of electrodes. All the while her body was shaking and jolting. Three types of spasm were identified. And then an even bigger discovery. A dystonic leg was diagnosed. The doctors were on to something. But the worst test of all was still to come: the myleogram.

The procedure involved injecting dye into the spine so that its passage up the spinal column and into the brain could be observed on monitor screens. Julie was strapped to a table which was tipped up to allow the dye to move freely up to her brain. She felt it enter her head and screamed. The liquid was moving around her head until it felt as if it must explode. This gruelling test left Julie drained and exhausted. But the doctors were excited. A definite diagnosis had been reached. She had dystonia.

Professor Marsden was not sure about the cause. Many metabolic, degenerative and environmental conditions can result in the symptoms; brain injury at birth, head trauma, toxic exposure to chemicals, even wasp stings. The professor knew that with Julie's history of injuries, illness and drug treatment, a chemical imbalance of the brain might have been sparked off.

Pain-relieving drugs were administered through a constant epidural drip but the effect was short-lived. Suddenly the whole of Julie's body was thrown into an enormous spasm. She thought she was going to die. Doctors blamed the drug going too quickly into her brain, but they weren't sure. Julie suspected the disease was spreading through her body.

More drugs were given, notably benzhexol and the L-dopa formula, but the dystonia had now taken hold. Strong spasms were beginning to attack her arms, shoulders, neck and chest. Her head started to turn to one side and drop down. It was mid summer. Julie had been in hospital for four months.

In desperation an experimental drug, botulinum toxin, was prescribed. It was a potent substance, manufactured at Porton Down, the former MOD microbiology establishment. There could be grim side-effects, but time was running out for Julie, so the toxin was injected into her body.

Autumn and winter passed. The toxin was working. By March the improvement in Julie's condition was significant, she was straighter than she had been in three years. But the poison was also taking its toll. 'People were horrified at the effects of the drug,' she says. 'I became weaker and thinner by the day, and they thought darkly that if I survived the dystonia I might well die of the treatment. The botulinum toxin seemed to be drawing me closer to death.'

Julie survived the spring but by summer her condition had deteriorated so much that she was taken into intensive care with severe breathing problems and malnutrition. Her body was hideously contorted, and for more than a week medical staff battled to stabilise her condition. Outside the hospital hundreds of caring people prayed.

At this time Canon Jim Glennon, an Australian Anglican minister with a ministry of healing, was paying a visit to London. Friends of Julie asked him to come and pray for her. He was moved by her story and agreed to visit the hospital on 14th June 1989.

'Very simply and with quiet authority he began to pray that my twisted body would be healed. I felt that I had been in the presence of someone special.'

A short time later, Julie felt able to sit up. The following day, with the help of crutches, she walked. For two days the healing continued, and then the cruellest blow: the body spasms returned with a vengeance. In one day she suffered four. On each occasion she felt as if her throat had a rope around it, and that something was crushing her chest.

'I thought I had crossed the last hurdle,' Julie says. 'But then I wondered why I wanted to stay in this world. I knew I had little more effort to give.'

Sixteen days had passed since Jim Glennon had prayed for Julie. Now it was 30 June and Professor Marsden suggested a last desperate resort: brain surgery. He didn't want to do it, but everything else had failed. The operation was called stereotactic surgery. It had only a 40 per cent chance of success and was extremely risky. It involved passing a probe with an electric current into the basal ganglia to 'fry' those areas of the brain in charge of abnormal movement. But while spasms might be stopped, all normal function in that area might also be destroyed. Damage and paralysis in other parts of the body were not uncommon following stereotactic surgery, the Professor admitted. 'And there is something else,' he said. 'Surgery must be carried out while the patient is conscious.'

Tom was horrified. 'There must be something else we can do,' he protested. 'I just can't let you do that to her.'

But the alternative seemed only marginally less appalling, and no more hopeful. All they could do, the Professor explained, was to knock Julie out completely with the antiepileptic drug clonazepam, give her a tracheotomy, and put her on a ventilator, 'cabbage-like'.

It was a bleak choice, but a decision had to be made quickly. The spasms were so violent that there was a real fear Julie's neck would be broken in the middle of an attack. A compromise was reached. The clonazepam dose would be increased further by drip, so that she was heavily sedated, but not so much that she needed to be ventilated.

For three days Julie just lay there, an inanimate, twisted form. But then something started to happen. She began to improve. The dose of clonazepam was reduced. Normal control returned to her limbs. Within a week she was discharged from hospital. Within two weeks she had thrown away her crutches. On 8 August 1989 Julie was paraded in front of Professor Marsden and all his students and fellow doctors and given a rousing cheer.

The Professor was amazed. In twenty-five years he had seen only one other severely affected victim of dystonia make such a recovery: a woman who visited Lourdes and was completely cured within a month of her return. Now he was looking at a woman who, within weeks of lying hideously contorted and close to death, was walking tall and poised without any hint of disability and full of life. By September Julie was off all drugs. The battle was over.

In August 1991 Julie received further prayer, during which the two fingers of her left hand, which had remained curled in, spontaneously straightened. Her healing was complete.

27

The Doctor and the Priest

SIROKI BRIEJ, CROATIA, 1995

The cancer had returned. It had been almost a year since Dr Therese Molinier had visited Father Jozo Zovko, seeking a miracle cure. Now the biopsy brought the news she did not want to hear: she would need to face more surgery, and the possibility of losing her vocal chords. Maybe God had not heard Father Zovko's prayer. Maybe there was not going to be a miracle cure. Maybe she would die.

Therese Molinier, a compassionate and gifted doctor of medicine, contracted cancer of the throat in 1985. She had a course of radio-therapy, but the cancer reappeared a year later. She was forty-seven years old at the time and recalls: 'I had an operation to remove the cancer, but luckily I did not lose my vocal chords. But as a result of the operation swallowing even the smallest piece of food became very difficult. I was just like a baby; everything had to be liquidised.'

Therese's suffering went on for seven years. Then, in October 1993, she and her husband, Jean-Claude, also a doctor, went to the monastery at Siroki Briej in Croatia to see Father Jozo Zovko, a Franciscan priest with a healing ministry.

'Both Jean-Claude and I are practising Catholics, but we were sceptical,' she says. 'We prayed with him, he laid his hand on my head, and then, during Mass, I asked God to make me just a little better. To my astonishment, when I was given the consecrated bread, it went down easily.

'It was 3.30 pm and I still had not eaten. So I went to our room in the guesthouse, made a bowl of mashed potatoes and ate them without any difficulty. Then I had an apple. Since then I have never had to use a liquidiser. I gave mine away that very afternoon! Because I had not chewed anything for seven years, the muscles of my throat had become weak, so it took time before they got back into shape, but now I can eat anything – fish, steak, sandwiches, whatever takes my fancy.'

Therese Molinier left the monastery believing she had been healed by God. Nine months later in July 1994, when a biopsy showed that the cancer had returned, she had enough faith to decide against vital surgery. Shortly afterwards, another biopsy revealed that she was completely clear of the cancer. She had not received any treatment.

'Jean-Claude and I have been astonished by the whole thing,' says Therese, 'as have my daughter and her husband. They are both doctors also, but what happened to me cannot be explained medically. It was simply an answer to a prayer, and we know in our hearts, as well as with our heads, that God really loves us.'

28

Angel Guard

SOUTH-EAST AUSTRALIA, 1992

He was a young boy in a world of fear and pain. He had moved to the small ocean town to stay but now wanted to get as far away as possible from the place his father called heaven, but which to him was more like hell. The first forty days had been okay, but then the dirt-bike gang started terrorising him, and after eighty days he couldn't take any more. He thought he would rather be dead.

The boy was fourteen, small and wiry, dark and good looking. His father was of Sicilian descent, although he had been born in Ireland. The boy's mother – 'More beautiful than any other woman in God's creation,' said his father – died when the boy was three. 'You have her eyes,' his father used to tell him. 'I wish she could see you now, and just what a handsome fellow you've grown to be.'

They had left Ireland in search of a better life. His father, a doctor, had accepted the offer of a job as medical consultant to a mining company near the small ocean town because he wanted to escape from the past, and the ghosts that haunted him there. There were too many sad memories in the place where he had married and then lost his wife. He thought moving to Australia would be good for him and the boy.

The small ocean town was beautiful; paradise compared to the depressing old city they had left behind. Their house had a beach instead of a front garden, and from his bedroom balcony the boy could see dolphins playing among the waves. The sun shone even on Christmas Day, and even the rain felt warm. In such surroundings the boy had not felt homesick for very long.

He liked going to the church. It wasn't like the drab building he and his father used to attend in Ireland, with its boring preachers and boring sermons. This place was so different. He liked the way they held the services outside in the summer, and that you could hear the wild birds calling when you sat inside, silent during the time of prayer. He certainly liked the girls in the choir – so much prettier than the girls back home – and the preacher's flowery shirt; better to look at than the vicar's black coat.

He had hated the thought of leaving Ireland, especially his friends and the house where he was born, but now he was glad to be living in the small ocean town, where the sea breezes made the curtains dance in the morning; and the afternoon sun lulled you to sleep, soothing away your cares. Yes, this new life was very, very good. But then it all turned bad.

The bikies, as the locals called them, were older than the boy – perhaps sixteen or seventeen – and lived on the other side of town. It seemed they had nothing better to do than tear along the streets and fire tracks, smashing mailboxes with baseball bats. They were always in trouble, and nearly always managed to squirm out of it. The local sheriff warned them when things started to get out of hand, but most of the time he ignored them. 'Bad boys, but harmless,' he told the doctor after the first time they had picked on his son. 'They're just trying it on. With your son being new in town and all that, they're trying to intimidate him.'

They had succeeded. The boy was not likely to forget the attack – or prank, as the sheriff viewed it. One of the bikies had ridden past the boy as he walked home from school one afternoon and snatched his bag. The strap had been over the boy's shoulder and the boy had been yanked to the ground and dragged a short distance along the road before the strap broke free.

The sheriff had promised to 'have a word' with the parents of the guilty party to 'make sure it doesn't happen again'.

It happened again. This time the boy was punched in the face for 'staring' at a member of the gang. By the time he got home his cheek and eye were bruised black and blue. He had been threatened with a beating if he grassed, so the story the doctor heard involved a playground scuffle during a game of football. And so it began: the bullying, the lies, the fear.

One day the dirt-bike gang trapped the boy in an alley and tried to force his hand into a sack that held a snake. When they failed they gave up and emptied the sack over his head, hoping the snake would attack him as it fell. But the boy was too quick and ran off. He cried all the way home. By the time his father returned he'd cleaned himself up.

'Good day at school? No more trouble with those yobs?'

The boy just shook his head, his eyes firmly fixed on the television screen. Inside he was trembling with fear, but he didn't show it.

He didn't show it after they held his hand palm-down on a log and took it in turns to stab a hunting knife repeatedly between his splayed fingers. He wasn't hurt, but he was scared enough to throw up on the way home.

The next time he was shot at. One of the gang rode past and fired at him with an air pistol. The pellet cut his ear but he told his father it happened playing rugby.

For the next two weeks they left him alone, riding past and not even glancing in his direction. He would see them laughing and joking with other kids after school and at weekends, and they would ignore him. At last he felt they had grown tired of their malicious game. But that was just what they wanted him to think.

It was all part of the torture. He realised that when the attacks started up again.

The bikies came screaming out of a back street, fists flying, boots kicking, machines roaring. It was all over in less than a minute and he was left lying in the gutter, bleeding and sobbing.

They would have come back to give him a kicking but they thought they'd seen someone watching. They had, but the woman only saw the gang riding away and by the time the sheriff came out she couldn't even remember the colour of the bikes.

'I'm sorry,' the sheriff told the boy's father. 'She's eighty years old and has failing eyesight. She heard the noise of the bikes, but by the time she got out to the street they were way down the road.'

The doctor grunted irritably and said he would ask the woman if she'd remembered anything else when he saw her at church.

'Meanwhile there must be something you can do, sheriff. You know who they are – and if *you* won't do something, *I* will.'

'Let me tell you something,' the sheriff growled. 'One: you don't go taking the law into your own hands. Two: we don't have any proof they were the same boys who tried to snatch his bag. So leave it.'

The doctor turned to his son, his cheeks flushed. 'Are you sure you didn't see their faces? It was broad daylight, for goodness' sake.'

'No,' said the boy.

The sheriff raised his voice. 'Is that, no you are not sure, or no you didn't see them?'

'No, I didn't see them.'

Perhaps it was fear, perhaps a little pride, but the boy would not tell, even though he knew they would already be planning their next attack. He knew, too, that he did not want to go on living in a world full of pain and fear. He did not believe the bullying would stop and could think of only one way out. He hoped God would forgive him.

But God had another solution planned.

The gang picked on the boy just three more times, and then the bullying stopped. The old woman was not surprised. She saw the boy as she was leaving the church one Sunday and sat next to him.

'I'm glad your little problem has gone away,' she whispered. 'I asked God to send you an angel, to watch out for you. I hope you don't mind.'

He did not know what to say and just looked at her, puzzled.

'Don't worry,' she said, smiling. 'It's our secret, just between you, me and God. He sometimes works in mysterious ways; ways we don't understand. But you can be certain those awful boys won't trouble you again. They wouldn't dare.'

Now the boy was smiling too. 'Thank you.'

She squeezed his hand again and got to her feet.

'Remember – it's our little secret.'

Three weeks passed before the boy realised what had happened. He couldn't stop thinking about what the old woman had said, but didn't understand it until one of the bikies pulled up outside his house one day.

'Hey, you,' he called as the boy was about to go inside. 'Come 'ere. I want to ask you something.'

The boy froze, for a moment, then looked up and down the street.

'It's okay, I'm on my own,' said the kid on the bike.

'What do you want?' the boy asked.

'I just want to . . . well, I want to say . . . I mean . . . sorry.'

The boy stared at him. 'Oh yeah?' Was this another of their tricks? But the kid on the bike looked awkward.

'We never meant no harm. We was just messin' about.'

'Just a game, was it?' The boy spat the words out.

'No, honest. We didn't mean nothin' by it.'

The boy noticed that the kid kept looking past him toward the house.

'What's up?' he asked. 'What are you looking at?'

The bikie was definitely uneasy. 'I was just making sure your mates aren't hangin' around. Your big brothers, are they?'

'What? I don't know what you're talking about.'

'Come on, you know what I mean.' The kid was getting agitated now. 'Your mates – the two of 'em who knock about with you all the time. Talk about bodyguards. There's a couple of the gang wanted to do you over again, but we said no way – not if you got mates like that. The bossman, he was gonna get you on the way home from school, but he changed his mind when those big guys showed up. I never seen him scared before.'

The boy was speechless. He'd been out on his own ever since he'd arrived in town. He had no brother and no mates – well, not big ones likely to put the wind up a bunch of dirt-bikers.

'Listen,' said the kid, 'I don't want no trouble. Like I said, I'm sorry we messed with you.'

The boy felt suddenly bolder and moved quickly toward the gate. The biker backed off and the boy loved it.

'Well, you'd better make sure it doesn't happen again, hadn't you?'

The kid nodded eagerly. 'Does this mean I don't have to worry about your mates beating up on me?'

The boy made him wait for an answer. 'I'll mention it to them. I'll let them decide.'

He watched the bikie take off down the road and stood scratching his head. 'Weird,' he said out loud. 'Totally weird.'

But the old lady didn't think so. Even when she saw the two angels walking down the street behind the boy she didn't think it was weird. They were wearing ordinary clothes. *But then they would*, she thought. *Wings and shining swords would look out of place!*

They were well over seven feet tall, well built, perfectly proportioned. One was fair, the other dark. 'My, they are handsome, Lord,' she whispered as they passed by her house. 'Thank you for answering my prayer.'

29

Wall of Death

MISSOURI, USA, 1990

Evan Wall's struggle for life began on 16th September 1990. Four months later he lay close to death. Doctors told Diane Wall there was no hope for her husband. When they called Evan's mother, they advised her to come at once if she wanted to see her son before he died. He was, by any reckoning, a hopeless case.

Evan, a forty-one-year-old hospital visitation pastor, had been rushed to St Mary's Health Center in Jefferson City, Missouri after suffering a massive stroke. Two weeks earlier he had been at St Mary's with Diane for the birth of Hannah, their fifth child. Now, in a cruel twist of fate, he was back again.

The stroke had affected Evan's left side, his co-ordination and his voice. His progress over the following three months was slow but eventually Evan was moved to another hospital for rehabilitation. On 7th December he was released. Diane and the children were overjoyed, but their relief and happiness were to be short-lived.

Over Christmas Evan experienced severe back pains. He couldn't sleep and grew so weak he finally collapsed. An ambulance rushed him back to hospital on New Year's Day. He had lost three quarters of his blood, almost haemorrhaging to death. One doctor told him that if he had gone one more day, maybe even half a day, he would have died of heart failure.

And things got worse. A new problem developed. A fistula, an abnormal passage, had formed over a ten- to fifteen-year period, causing stomach acid to seep through a faulty valve in Evan's oesophagus. By the time the doctors diagnosed the problem it had burned a hole through the oesophagus, causing bleeding. Evan needed immediate surgery.

But the night before the scheduled operation, Evan's doctor walked into his room and told him: 'We can't perform surgery on you. We've got a problem. The lab checked and double-checked the blood tests and found that you've contracted HIV, the AIDS virus.'

Evan was distraught. 'I'm a heterosexual,' he told the doctor. 'And I was a virgin when I married my wife. The only way I could have contracted HIV would have been from a blood transfusion.'

The doctor had already informed Diane. He told her Evan would have a month, a year, maybe five years, but would die of AIDS eventually. 'It was the worst call of my life,' she recalls. 'They said there was no hope for him, no hope at all.'

On 17th January 1991 doctors decided to go ahead and operate on Evan. Surgery lasted seven hours. Afterwards hopes were high until disaster struck yet again. Evan's heart failed first. Then his kidneys. They put him on dialysis, but that failed too. His lungs, heart rate and blood pressure were showing bad signs. Diane prepared herself for the worst. 'They told me he was as good as dead.'

Prayer lines at Evan's church were set up. It was a last hope. His name was broadcast over a local Christian radio station and his mother and father made it to the hospital. 'They didn't know about the miracle-working power of Jesus,' Evan says, 'but Mum challenged the Lord: "God, if there's a change in Evan we will go to church."' God must have heard that prayer because the dialysis began to work.

Evan's parents kept their promise and after thirteen days he was transferred out of the intensive care unit and hooked up to machines that carried out a second batch of blood tests. Evan was now reasoning with God. 'If what I believe is true – that you spared my life three times, once from the stroke, once from the bleeding to death at home, and once from my surgery when I went into complete body failure – then I don't believe you would have me die of a virus I picked up by accident.'

Evan believed God was going to do something miraculous with the secondary blood tests. 'My faith was being severely tested,' he says. 'Every time the nurses walked into my room with protective gloves on their hands it felt like my faith was being destroyed. But I knew God was going to do something good.'

Five blood tests were carried out at three major laboratories. Days passed and Evan grew anxious. The first test came back. It was negative. Within the next two weeks all five tests came back negative. For a while Evan wondered if he'd had the AIDS virus in the first place. But his doctor was certain. 'There is no mistake,' he told Evan. 'When you've got it, you've got it.'

One of the tests carried out, the 'Western blot,' searched for the AIDS virus exclusively. When it came back negative, the specialists were stunned. One of them told Evan's doctor that he had never seen one of those tests change from positive to negative.

'Doctor,' Evan said, 'when you are healed, you are healed.'

30

Soul Music

TYLER, EAST TEXAS, 1980

It was a cold night and George Bock was driving a rented black Ford along the deserted backstreets of downtown Tyler. The window was open and George felt the icy chill on his face. The air was still and peaceful like the moon, its pale light tinting the edge of the high clouds that drifted slowly across the winter sky.

For a moment, George turned on the radio, a slide guitar eased its way lazily into a bluesy country ballad. George took a right turn and drove the Ford down a narrow alley, across railroad tracks toward two scrap freight trucks standing on waste-ground.

He stopped the car, parking close to one of the trucks, and turned off the engine. He took a deep breath, closed his eyes and listened to the engine tick as it cooled. The silence made his ears hum. 'It is time,' he thought, opening his eyes and feeling for the black bag on the back seat. Inside was a gun, and George noticed how cold the metal was as he pulled out the weapon and placed it on his lap.

George Bock was planning to kill himself. A week earlier his wife and two small children had been killed in a road accident. Now he wanted to take his own life because he believed he could not live without them. He wound up the window, picked up the gun, loaded it with one bullet, opened his mouth and, feeling the

tension of the trigger against his finger, trembled as he slid the barrel between his teeth.

A dog barked and George thought it would be the last sound he would ever hear. But as he squeezed the trigger he heard another sound. Someone was singing; a lone female voice. George listened, his hand quivering. The singing continued and he hesitated. He tried to swallow, but his mouth was dry and the bitter-hard taste of the metal made him heave.

The voice became clearer, the words of the hymm familiar.

> Amazing grace! how sweet the sound

George eased back on the trigger. He wanted to die but took the gun out of his mouth. He held the weapon loosely on his lap and closed his eyes, resting for a moment beneath the shroud of sound; the voice permeating the very fibre of his being. The icy chill bit like razor-wire, and the coldness in his heart hurt. But as George listened to the hymm, a gentle warmth embraced him. He opened his eyes and looked out of the window and into the darkness. The sound was coming from somewhere close by. He listened intently, trying to home in on the source.

> That saved a wretch like me;
> I once was lost but now am found,
> Was blind, but now I see.

The words were clear. 'She must be standing behind the freight trucks,' he thought, stroking the gun with his thumb. 'Who is she, what is she doing here?' George asked himself, reaching for the black bag and dropping the gun inside. 'She must have heard the car, she must know I'm here.'

He was shaking now, with fear. 'So close, so close,' he whispered, 'so close to killing the pain.' With one of his big, shaking hands George opened the door and got out. He rested his tall, stocky body against the car. She was still singing, and with a heavy sigh George moved clumsily toward where he thought he would find the owner of the voice. He was no longer warm and the cold air made him shiver as he made his way toward the nearest freight truck.

George Bock could not understand why anyone would be here in this part of town, especially a woman, and at night. 'Maybe she's a drunk,' he thought, 'a drunken hobo, looking for shelter.'

But the sweet melody belied his conclusion and, even though George Bock became angry as he stumbled around in the darkness, something deep inside told him that this woman may have just saved his life. Despite that, as he walked toward the freight truck, plans for a second suicide attempt were already on his troubled mind.

The singing continued as he felt his way along the side of the freight wagon. Broken glass and discarded beer cans crunched under his shoes. He could smell oil, and smoke, and as he crossed behind the rear of the freight wagon, he saw flames. Someone was standing in the middle of an open expanse of wasteground, warming themselves in front of a blazing fire. But it was a man, and he was not singing. George Bock accidentally kicked a can and the noise ran out. He stopped, standing perfectly still, his breath billowing out like smoke from a steam train. The man, dressed in rags, looked over his shoulder but only for a moment, and went back to poking the fire with a stick.

Something on the fire popped, sounding like a gun shot. George was distracted for a moment, but the sound of the woman's voice, much clearer now, reminded him of his new purpose on this cold winter night. He listened again, searching the darkness, and spotted what appeared to be a deserted shack. It stood less than fifty yards away, leaning awkwardly on the edge of the wasteground, but barely visible in the shadow of a three-storey building.

George was sure the woman must be inside and he walked with greater urgency now, away from the freight trucks and the fire. The singing continued, but softer, and the words had been replaced by a soothing hum. He wondered if the man by the fire knew who was singing, and looked back over his shoulder but the fire was now unattended.

He stood close to the building. It wasn't just a run-down shack; it was an old wooden church, although apart from a wooden cross above the door, it resembled a large shed. Someone had smashed the glass in the windows and there was a hole in the roof where the tiles and felt had been removed. George turned up his collar and pushed his hands deep into his coat pockets. He shivered as he stood and listened.

The door was open but there was no light inside. George wondered how the sound had carried so far across the waste-ground, beyond the freight trucks and into his car. It didn't seem that loud now, but it was still powerful, intense, and he shivered again, but this time not from the cold.

She stood alone, a radiant figure, clothed in bright white robes. George stood just inside the door, silent, not daring to make a sound. She was still humming 'Amazing Grace' and beckoned to George to sit down on one of the dozen or so empty chairs, some of which were broken and upturned. He moved slowly and perched nervously on the edge of the nearest chair. She started the song again and George closed his eyes. The gentle warmth that first embraced him in the car returned and he began to cry.

Two weeks later George Bock was still alive. He sat in the rented black Ford outside the church; not the abandoned wooden church, but a shining, new building, with polished oak doors and stained glass, and a golden cross on a white marble monolith. The church where he hoped to find an answer to the burning question, lodged like a hot coal, in his heart.

He sat slumped forward, elbows resting on the steering wheel, head in his hands, palms pressing on his tired eyes. He had not had much sleep since the night he attempted suicide. The gun was still in the black bag locked in the dashboard compartment, exactly where George had left it before he searched for and found the mysterious woman, whose sweet voice had saved his life.

Now he asked himself the same question over and over again. Who is she? He had been back to the abandoned wooden church several times since, but she was nowhere to be seen, and a week after his first curious visit, the night when he stumbled through darkness to behold her angelic appearance, someone had burned the church to the ground. 'A demolition crew came in this morning,' a man walking a dog informed George, as he watched smoke rise from cooling ashes. 'They called it the timber chapel, it was there for years and years,' the man said.

'Who did it belong to?' asked George.

'Oh, I'm not sure who exactly, but they moved into a new place on the other side of town, last year I think. I guess the congregation got too big for that little old place.'

Now George stood outside the impressive oak door of the new church, waiting to meet someone he hoped could help him find the mystery woman. He was lost in tired, deep reflection, when he felt a gentle tap on his shoulder.

'Hello, I'm Father Delfante.' The tall, smiling man stroked his beard. 'I was expecting you.'

'Do I know you?' George asked, surprised at the greeting.

'No, you don't,' Father Delfante replied, 'but I have felt your pain and saw the angel who saved your life.'

George stood with his mouth open. He felt his legs weaken. 'Here, let me help you,' said the priest, putting his arm around

George and leading him inside the church. 'You must be a little confused.'

George looked at Father Delfante and nodded. He was speechless. They sat on a polished oak bench and George squeezed the bridge of his nose with his thumb and index finger, eyes tightly shut, trying to concentrate.

'Let me get this straight,' George said in whisper. 'You know what happened to me?' He looked at Father Delfante, who was nodding his head. 'You know everything?'

The priest put his arm around George, smiling. He scratched his beard. 'It is not the first time the angel has prevented someone from taking their own life. You are not the first, you may not be the last.

'About a year ago, I had a vision in which I saw a young woman standing on the edge of a tall building. She was going to jump because she did not want to live any more. I saw her step off the edge but her fall was broken in mid-flight by an angel who carried her to safety.

'Two days later a young lady came to see me. I recognised her as being the same girl I saw in the vision. She felt led to come to the church after attempting suicide. She told me she had jumped from the roof of the three-storey building, the same building that still stands on the site of our old wooden chapel, by the railway tracks.'

George felt uneasy. His pulse quickened. 'Are you okay?' asked Father Delfante. 'Do you want a drink of water?'

'No, please continue, I'm okay really, just a little shaky, that's all.'

'You have nothing to fear,' the priest continued, squeezing George's shoulder. 'About two weeks ago I had another vision.'

'Let me guess, you saw me trying to blow my head off with a gun,' George interrupted.

'Yes, that is true. And then I saw you walking in the darkness, looking for something. Someone was singing 'Amazing Grace', I recall, and you were following the sound, trying to find its source. And did you find what you were looking for?'

'Yes, yes I did,' George started to cry. 'I saw this beautiful woman inside the old wooden church and she was singing for me. She stood there and I just listened. I don't know how long for, or why, because I must have fallen asleep, right there, sitting inside that old church. And when I awoke she'd gone. I stayed there all night, nearly froze to death, but she didn't return. She saved my life, Father.'

'Yes, and your soul. Thank God for his angels.' Father Delfante stroked his beard and smiled. 'I trust you will be coming to church now,' he said. 'God has great plans for you, my friend.'

Two years later, George Bock, with the help of Father Delfante, established a mission in south-west Texas, near the Mexican border, its purpose to provide shelter and counselling for those who had lost loved ones. George Bock had the words 'Amazing Grace' carved in oak above the front door.

Bibliography

Chapter Three: Secret Cargo – adapted from *God's Smuggler*, Brother Andrew, Hodder and Stoughton

Chapter Twelve: Under the Cover of the Light – *The Hiding Place*; Corrie Ten Boom, Hodder and Stoughton

Chapter Fourteen: Under a Stormy Sky – *A Witness For Ever*, Michael Cassidy, Hodder and Stoughton

Chapter Fifteen: Rupe and the Preacher – *Nine O'Clock in the Morning*; Dennis J Bennett, Bridge/Kingsway

Chapter Twenty-three: Church on Fire – *When the Spirit Comes*; Colin Urquhart, Hodder and Stoughton

Chapter Twenty-six: Steps of Faith – *Dancer off her Feet*; Julie Sheldon, Hodder and Stoughton